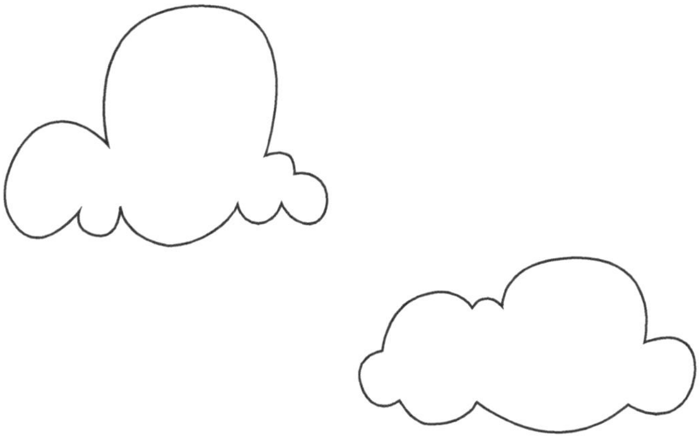

This Book Belongs To:

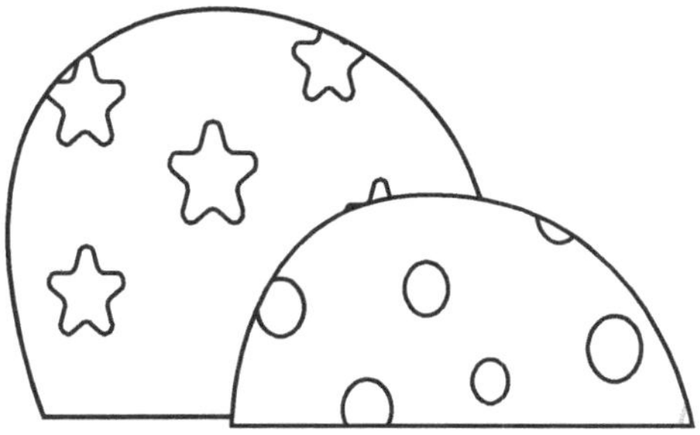

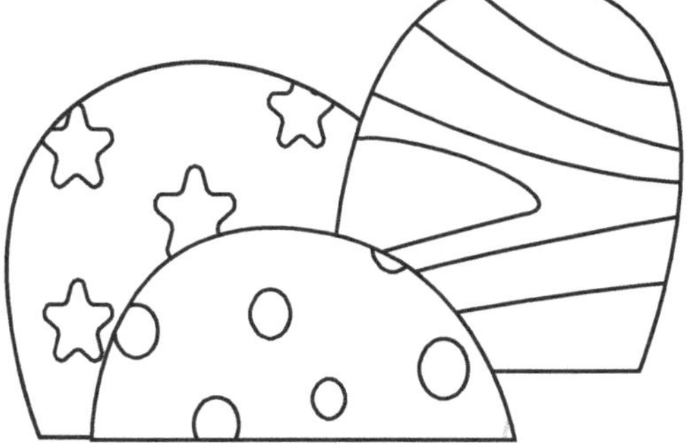

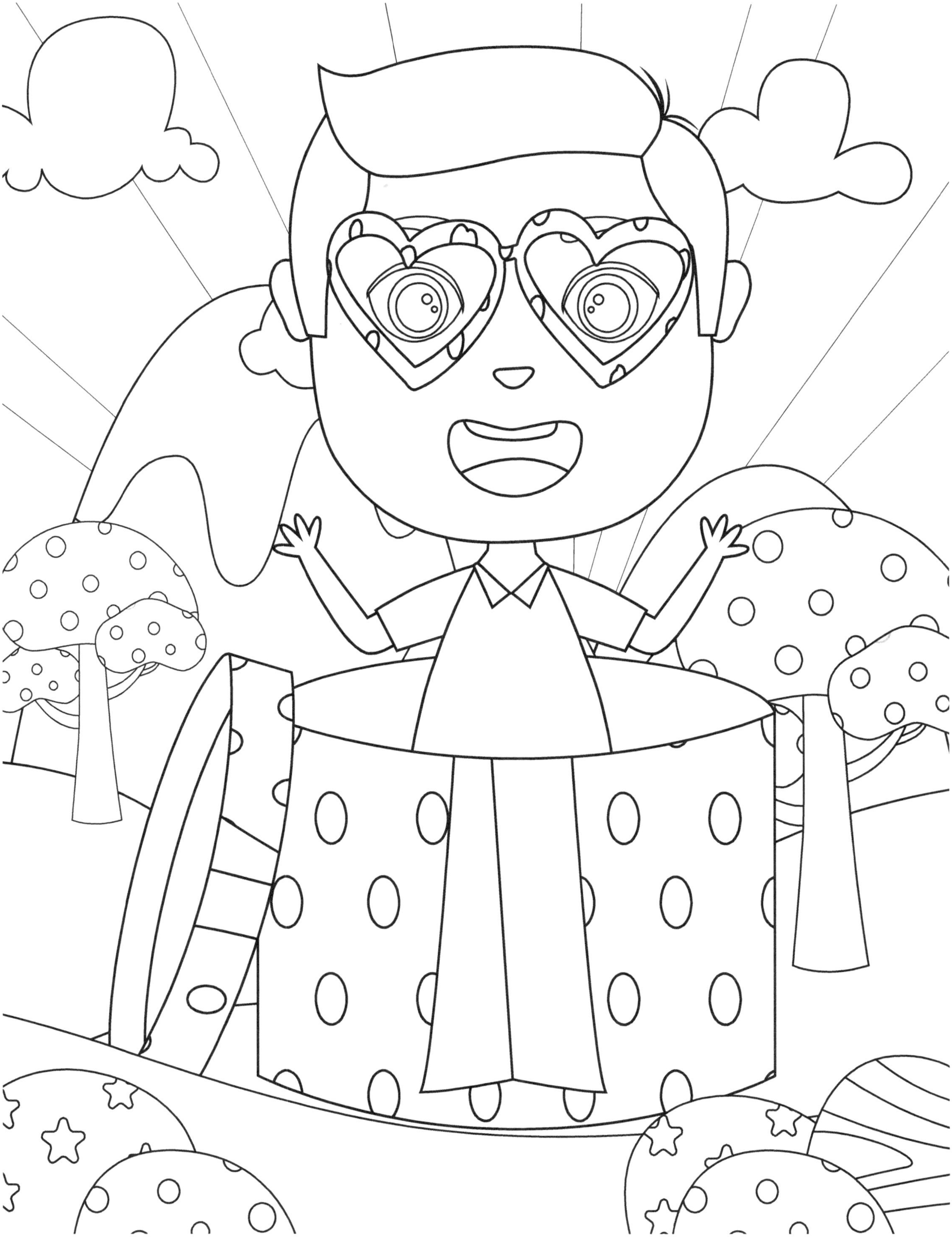

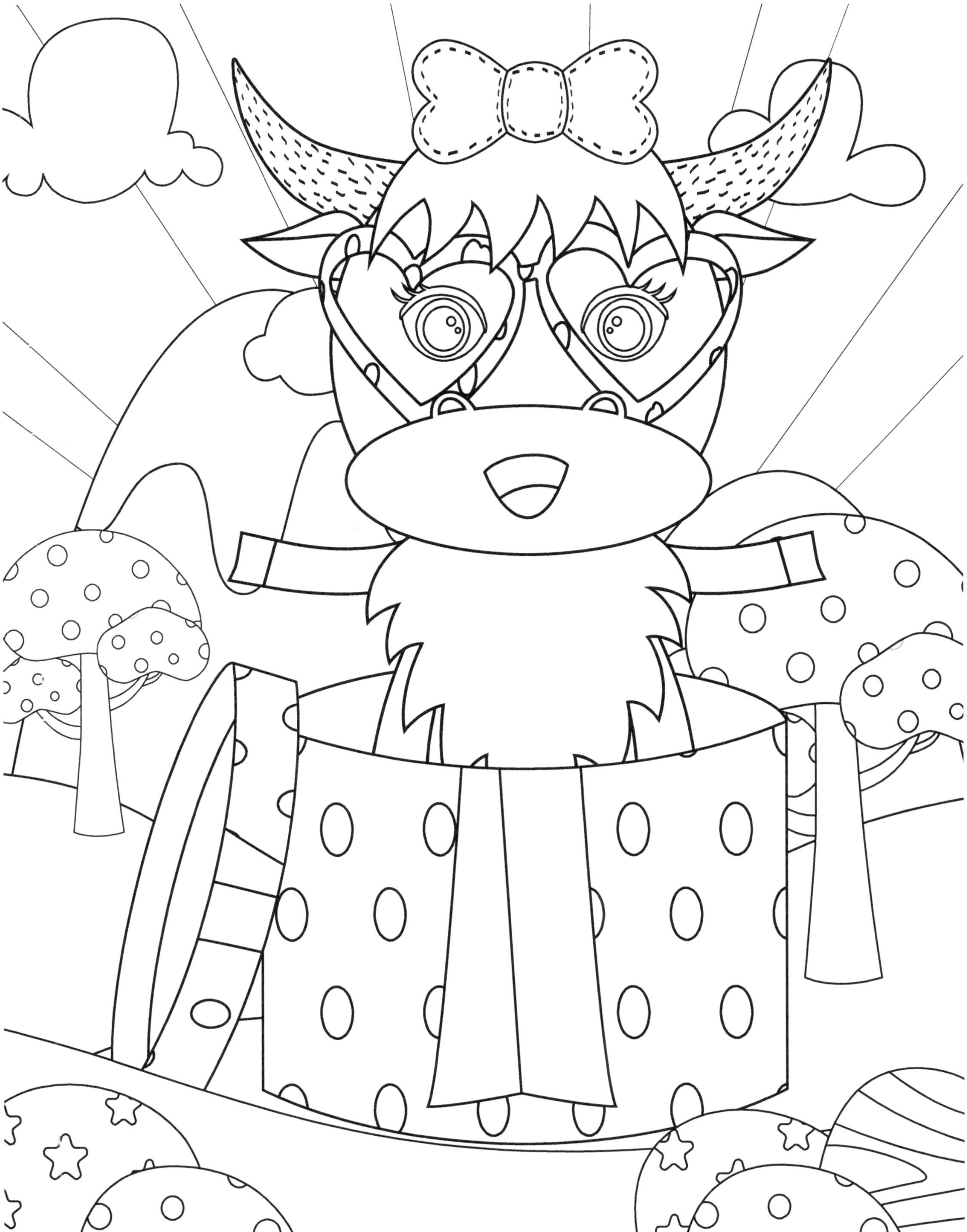

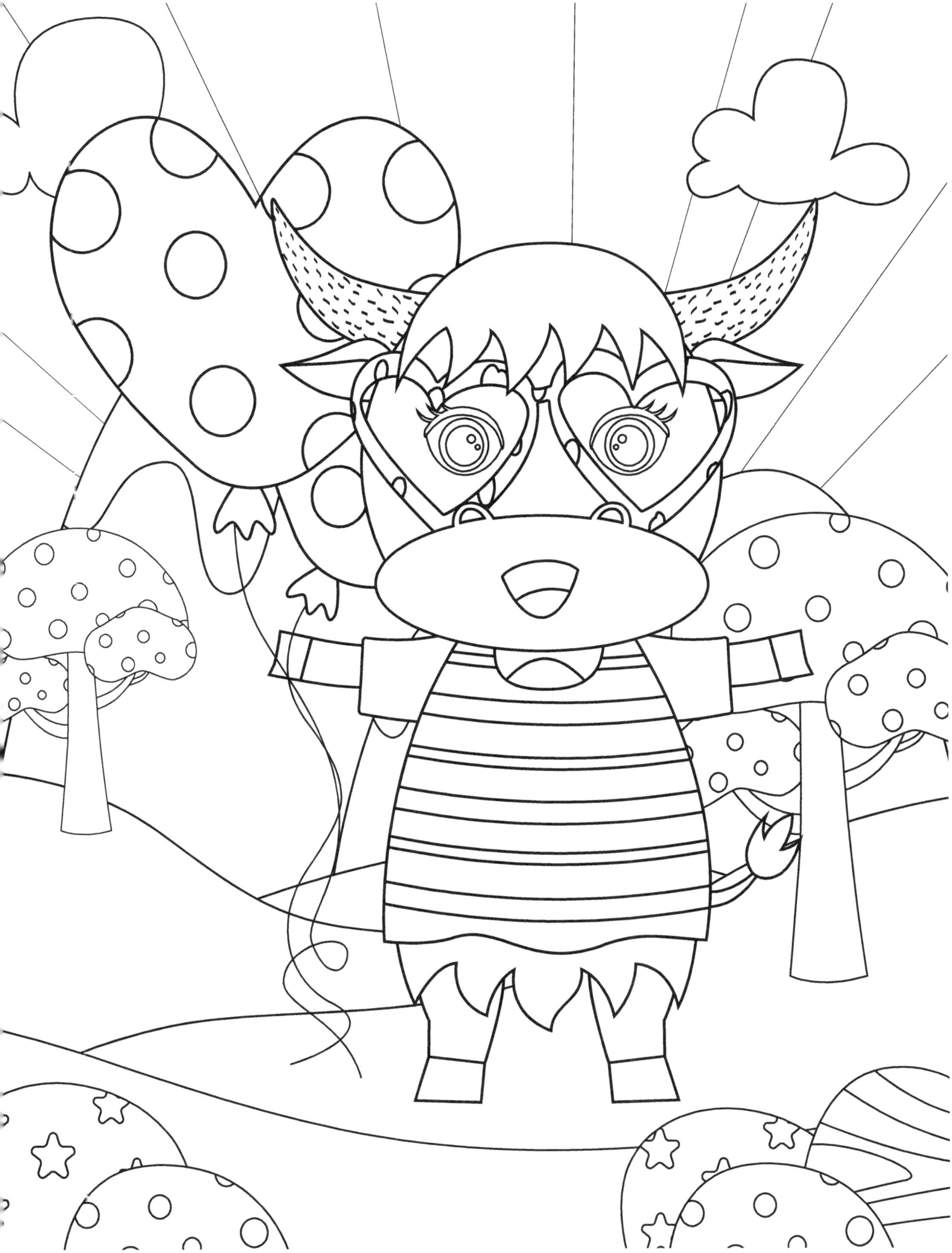

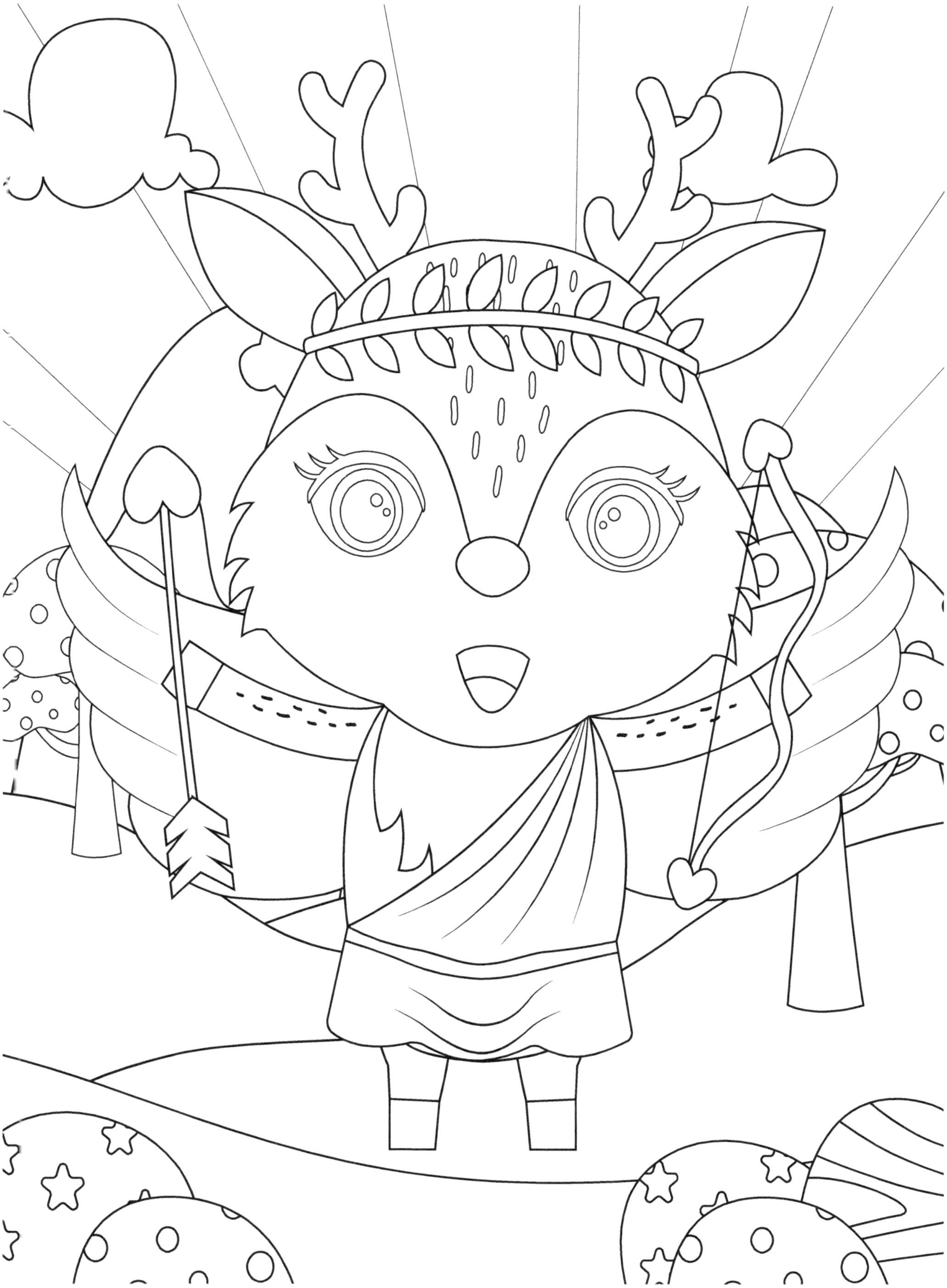

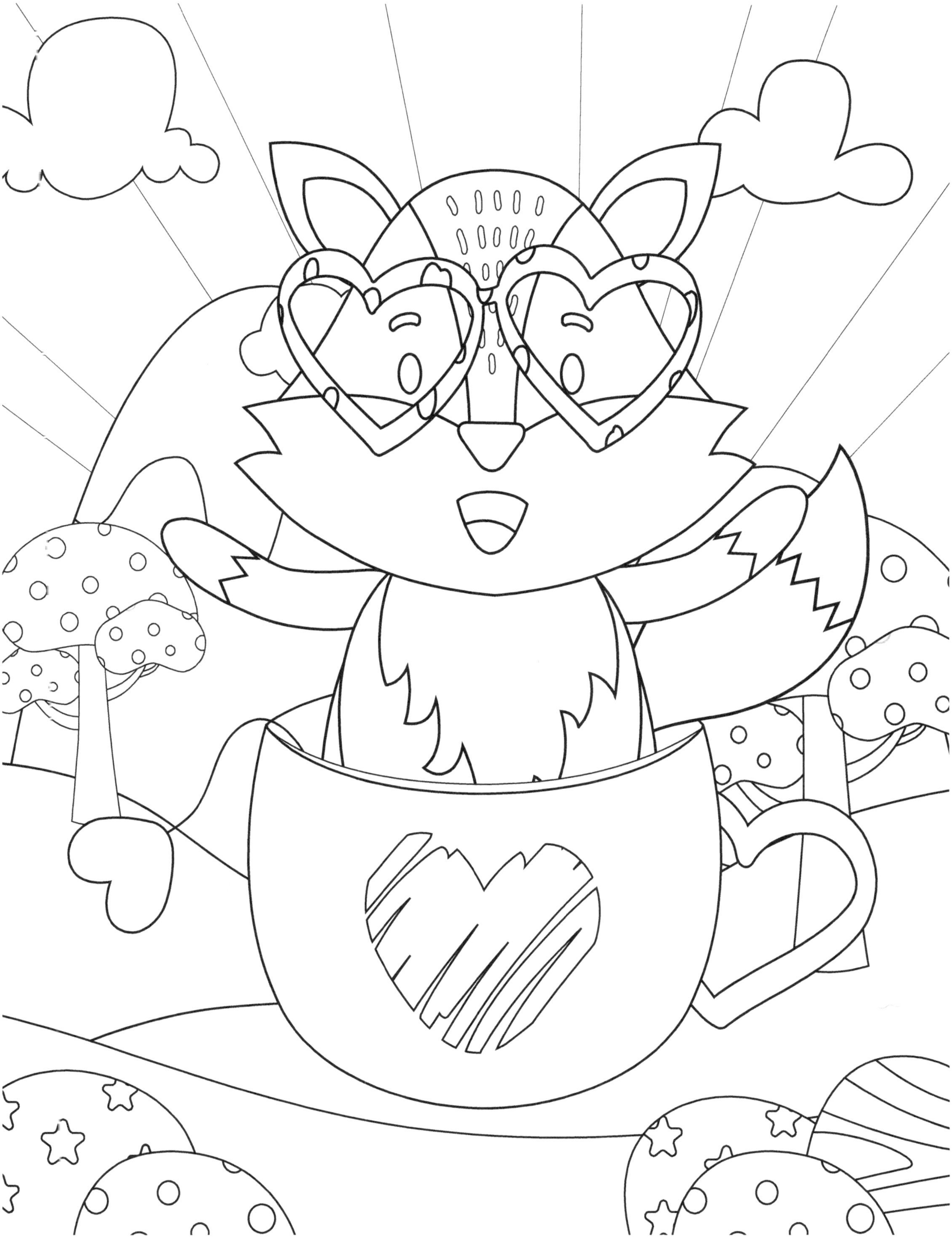

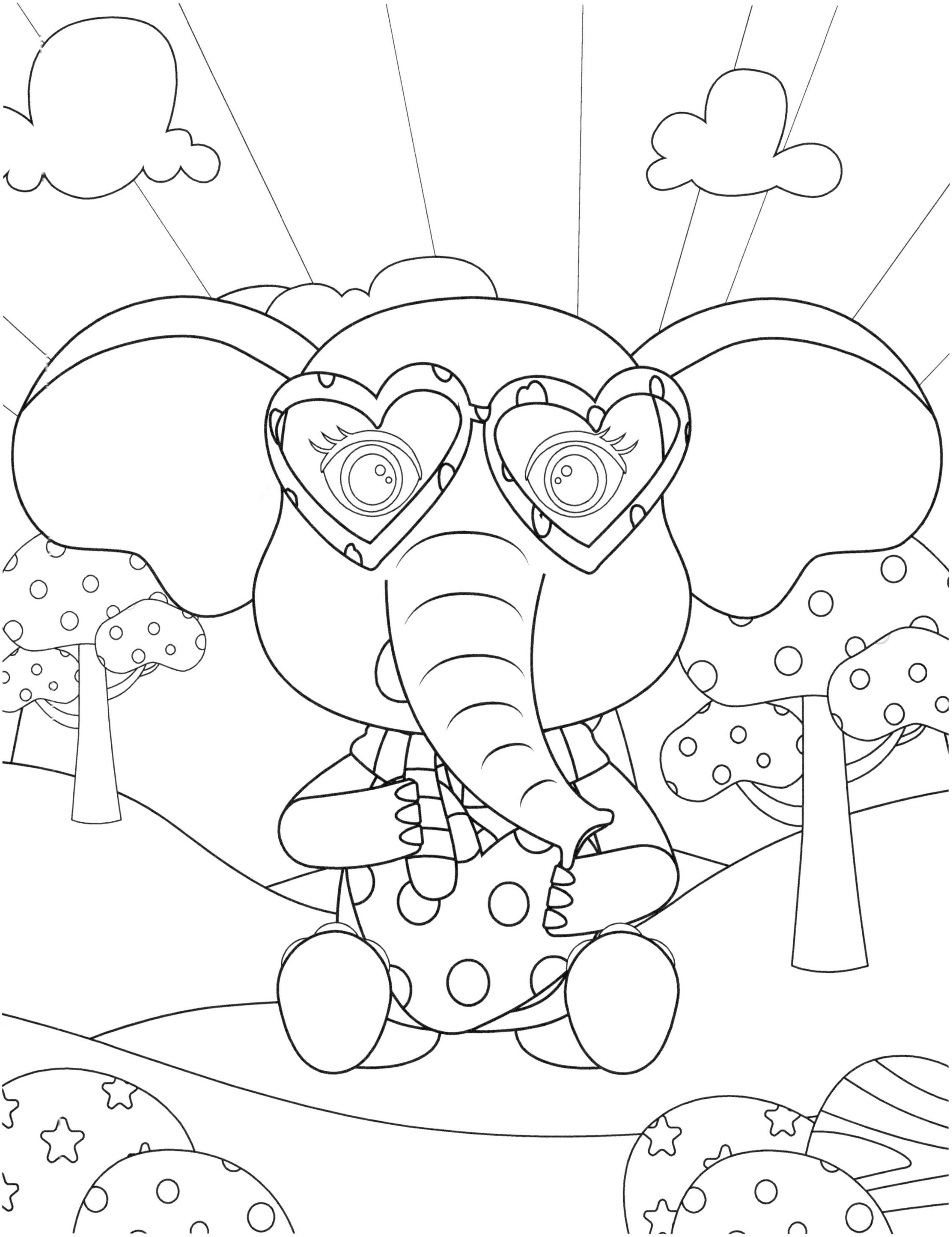

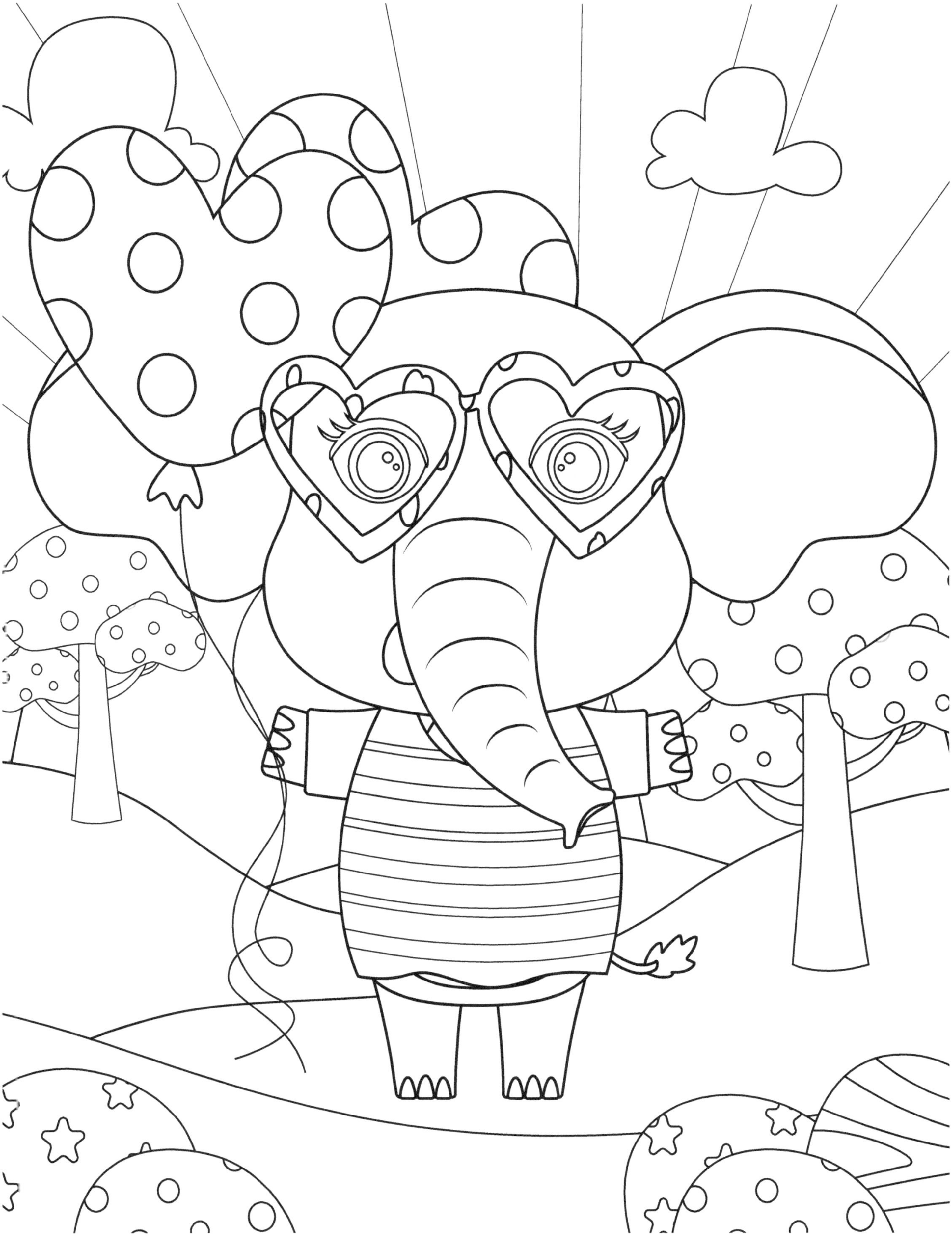

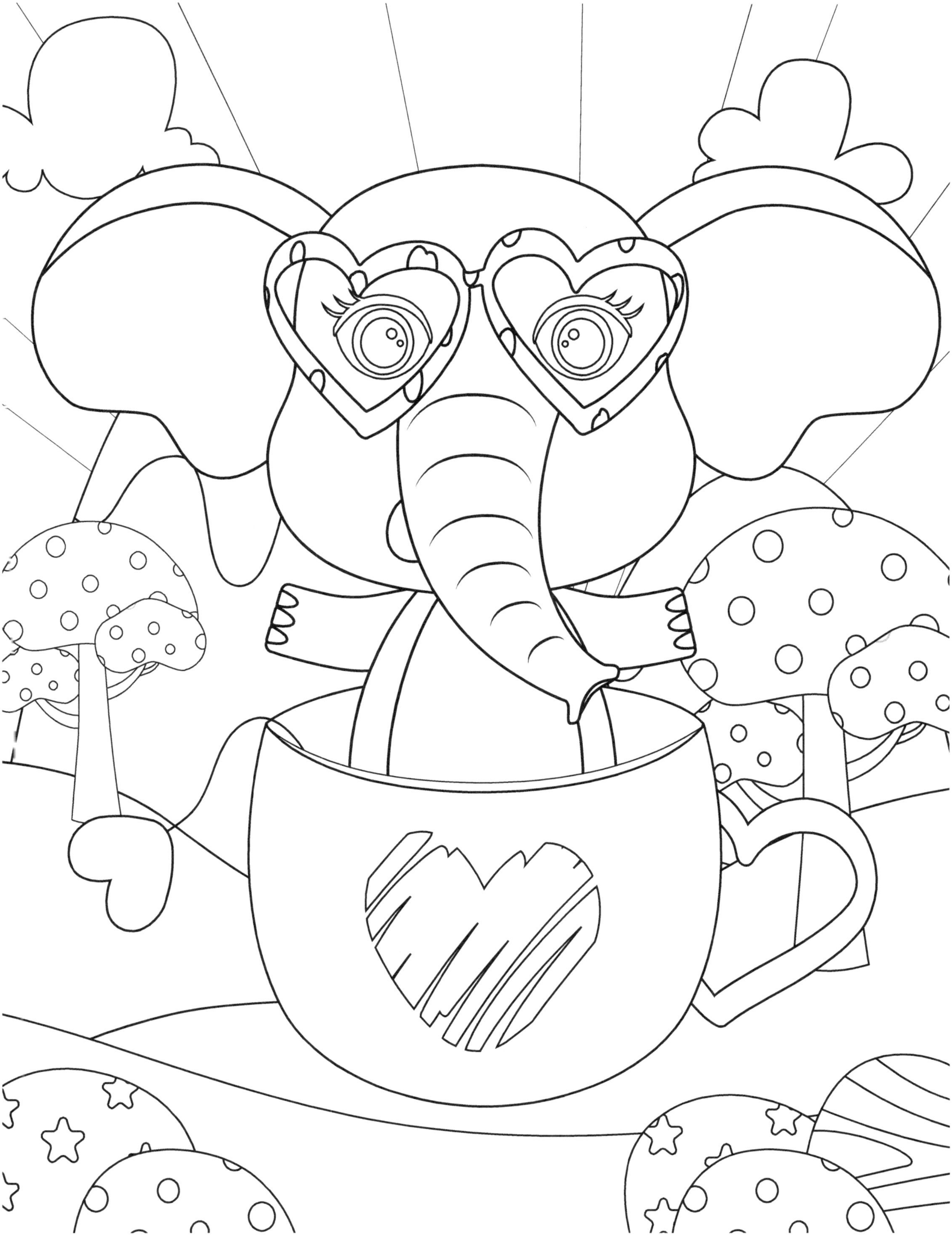

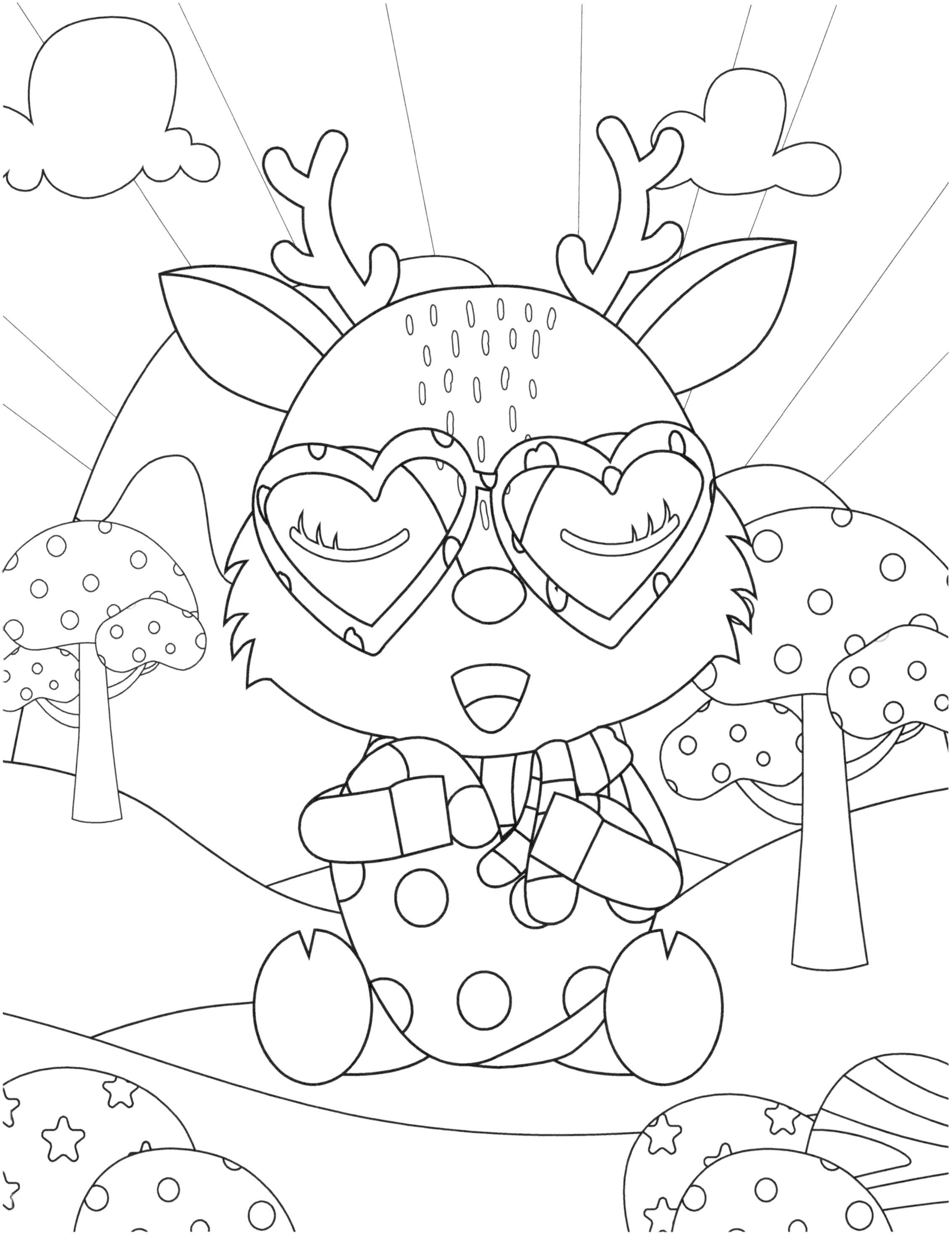

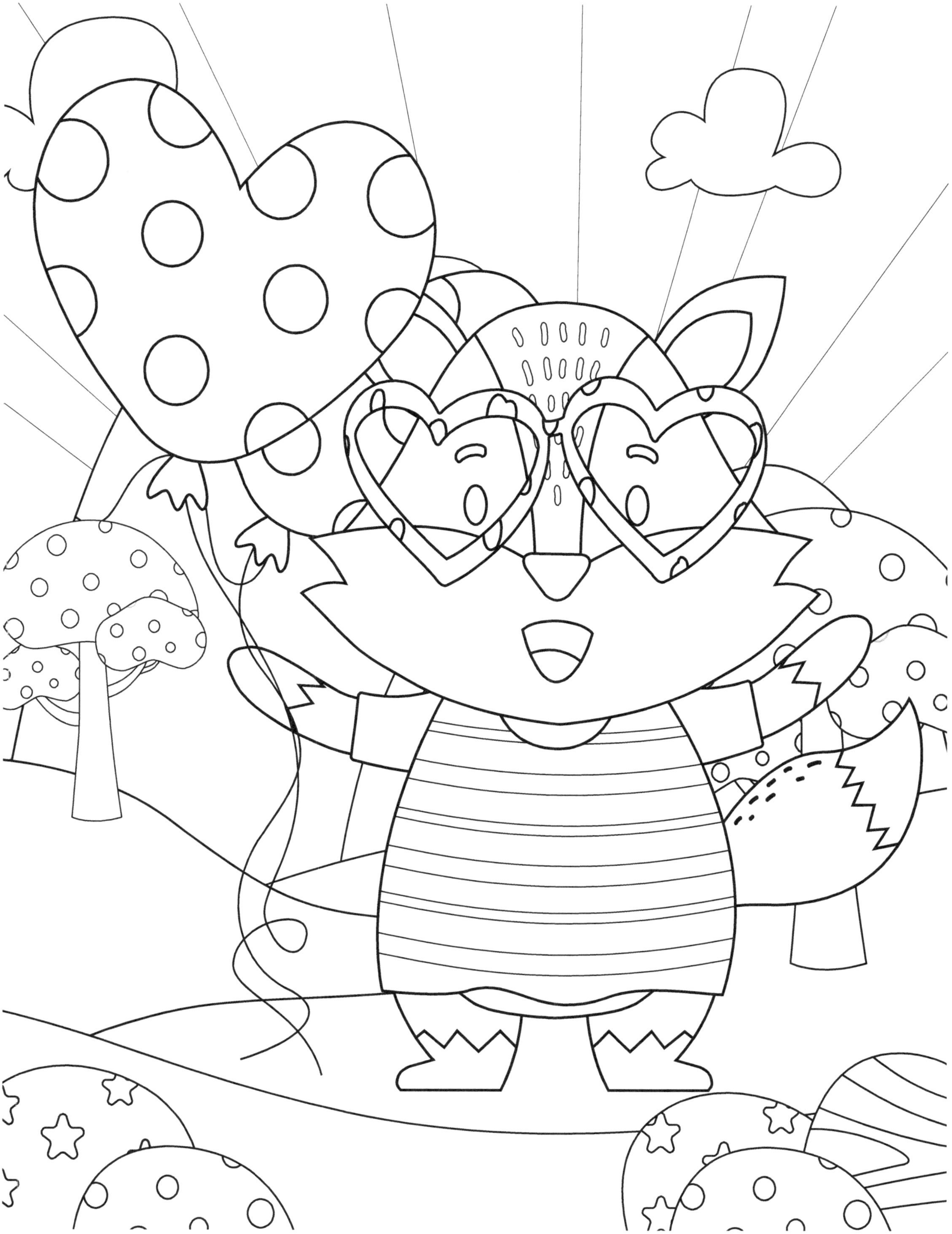

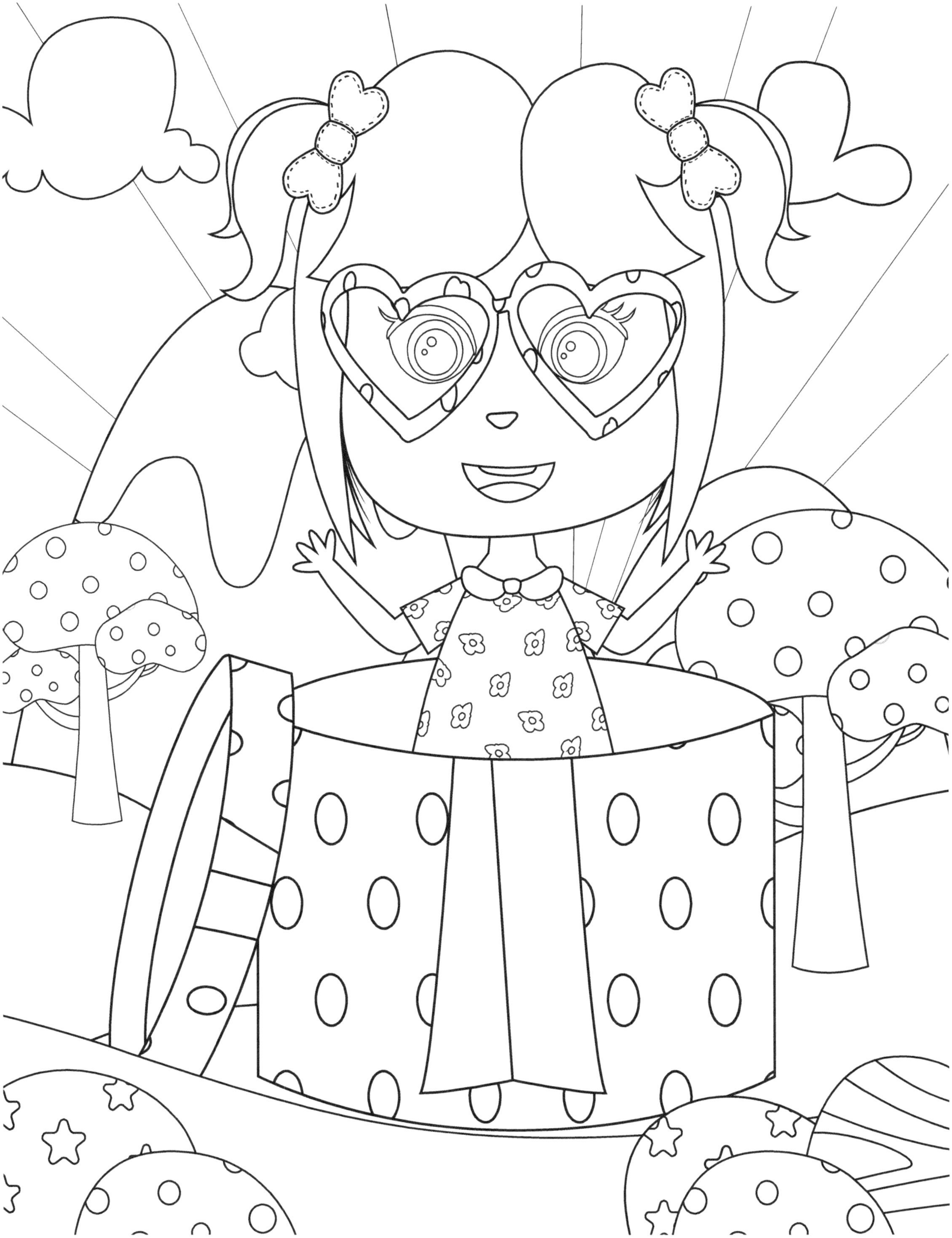

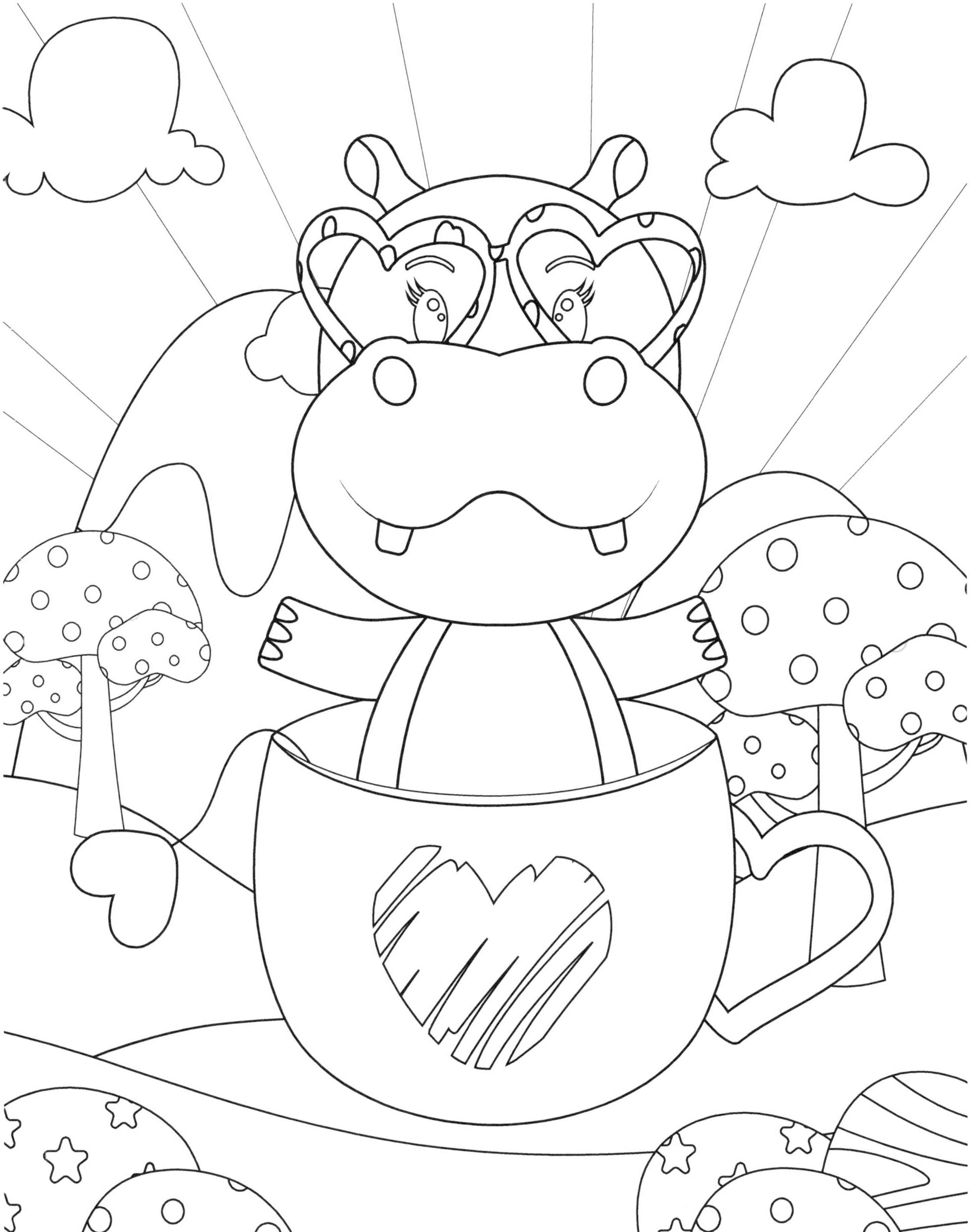

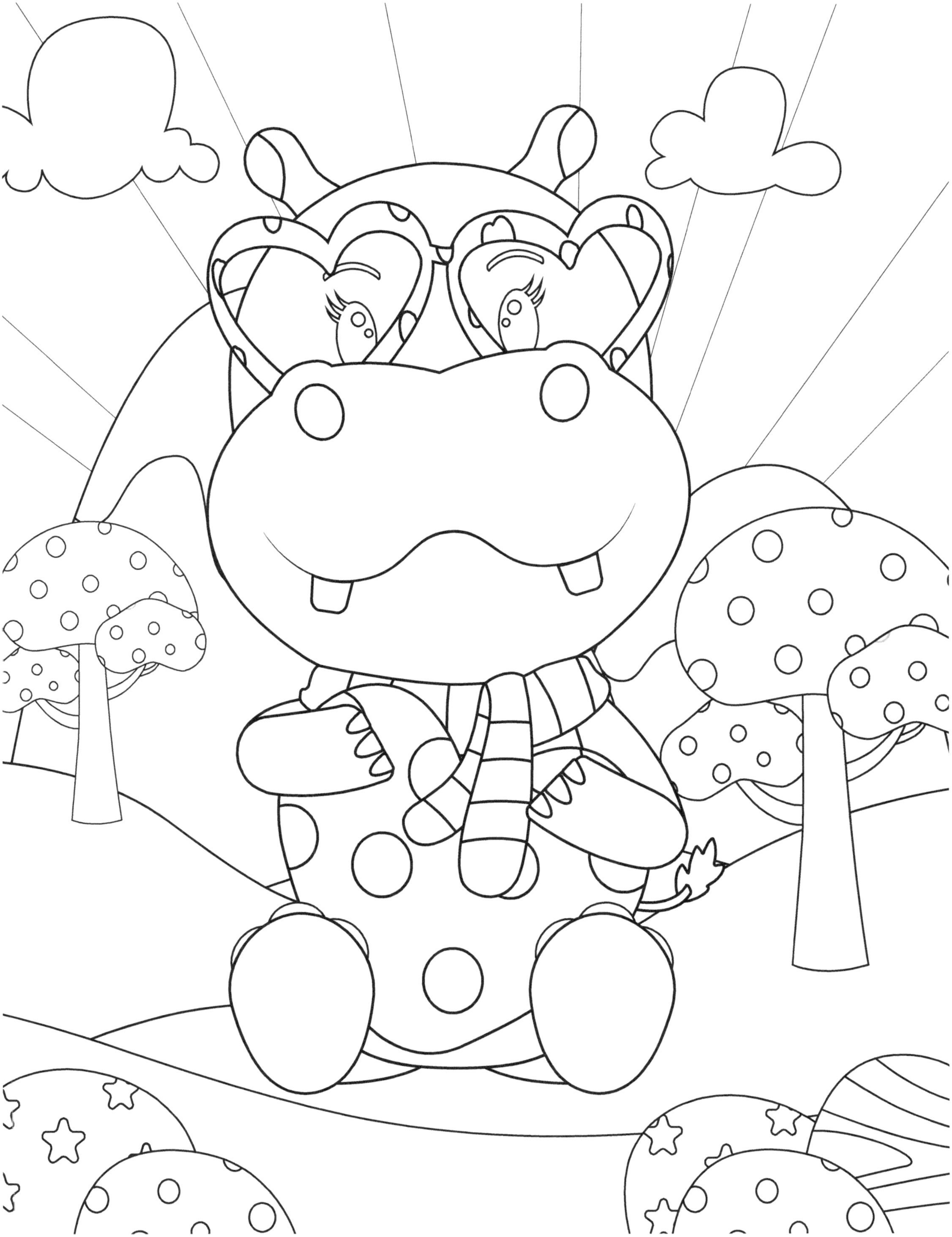

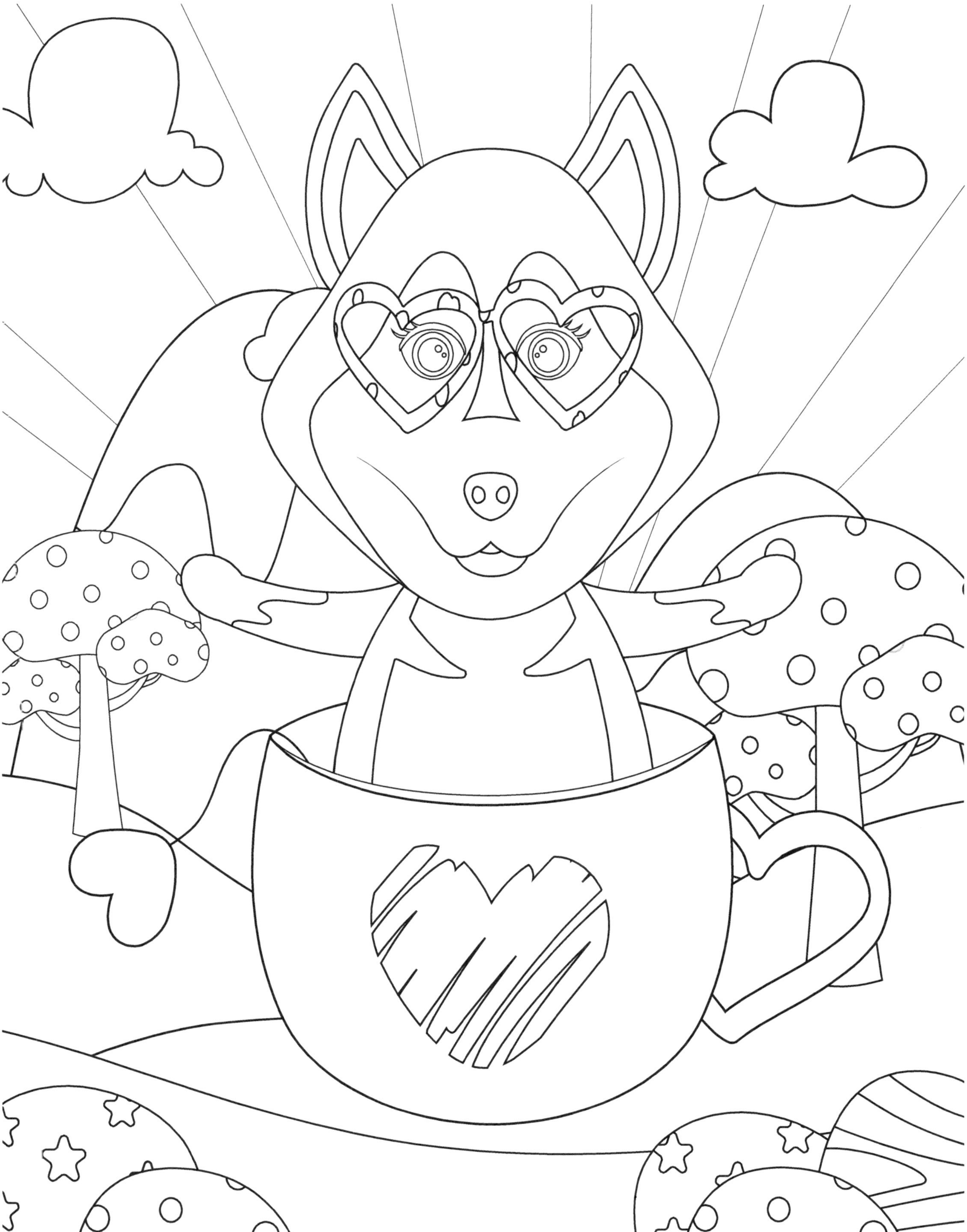

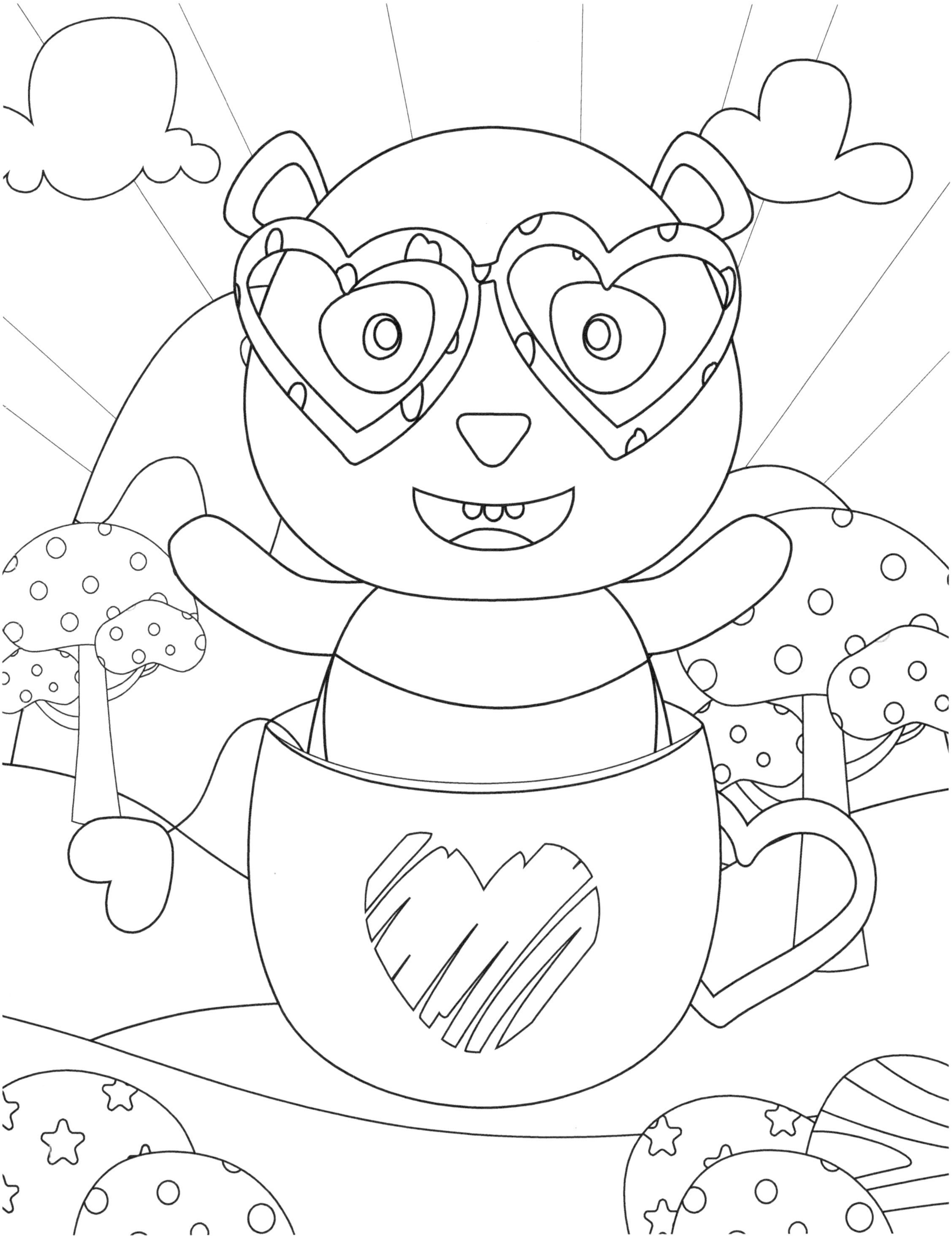

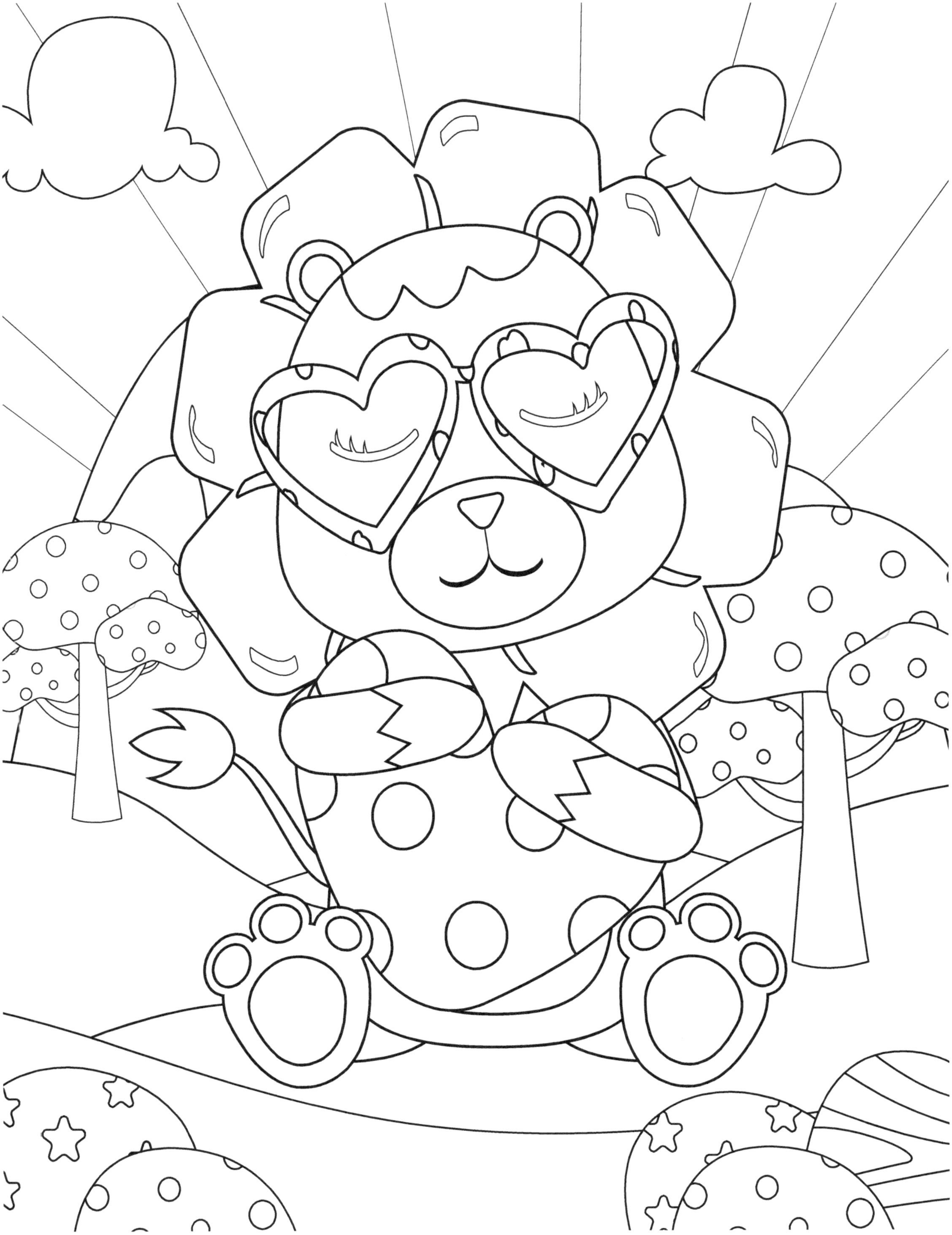

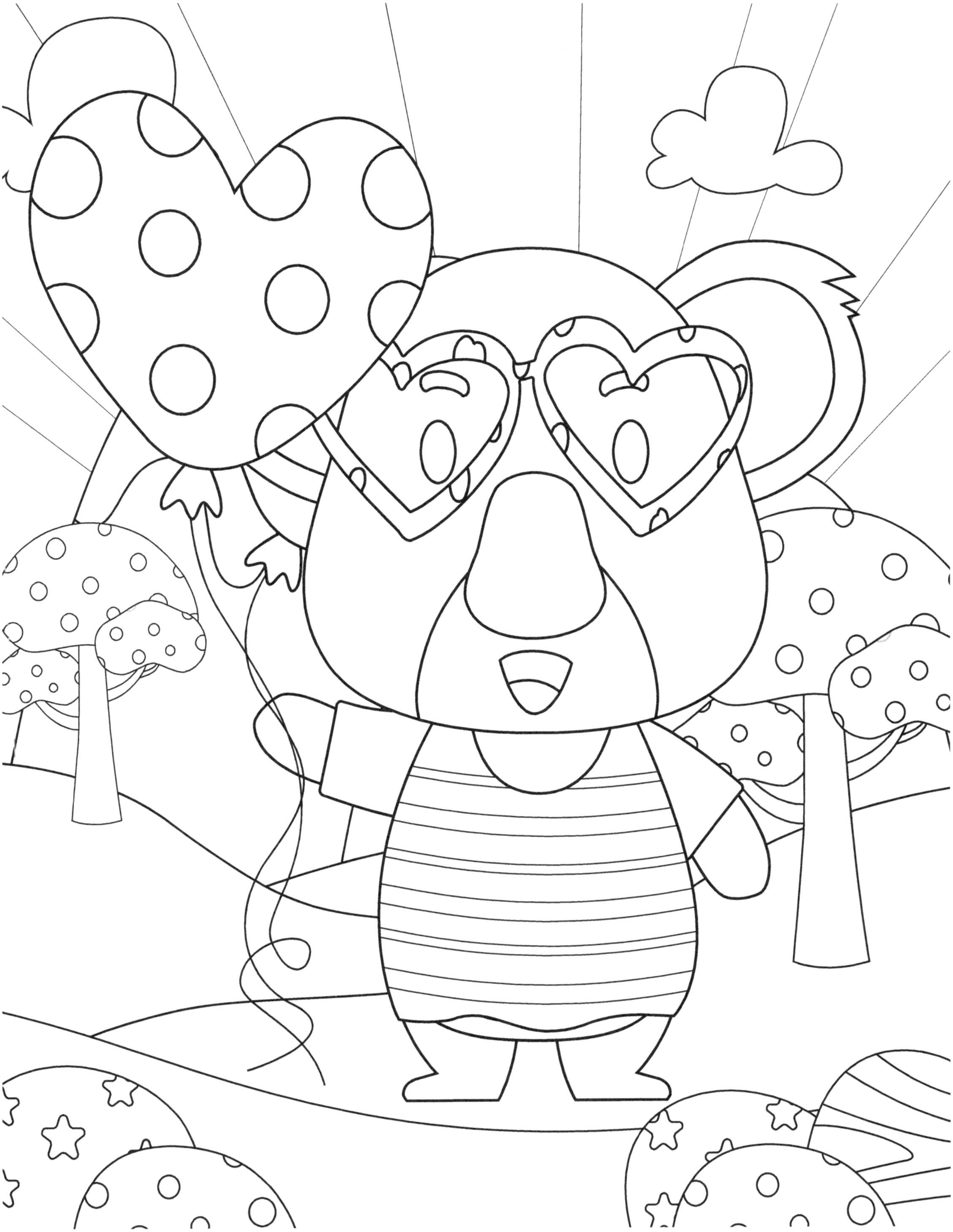

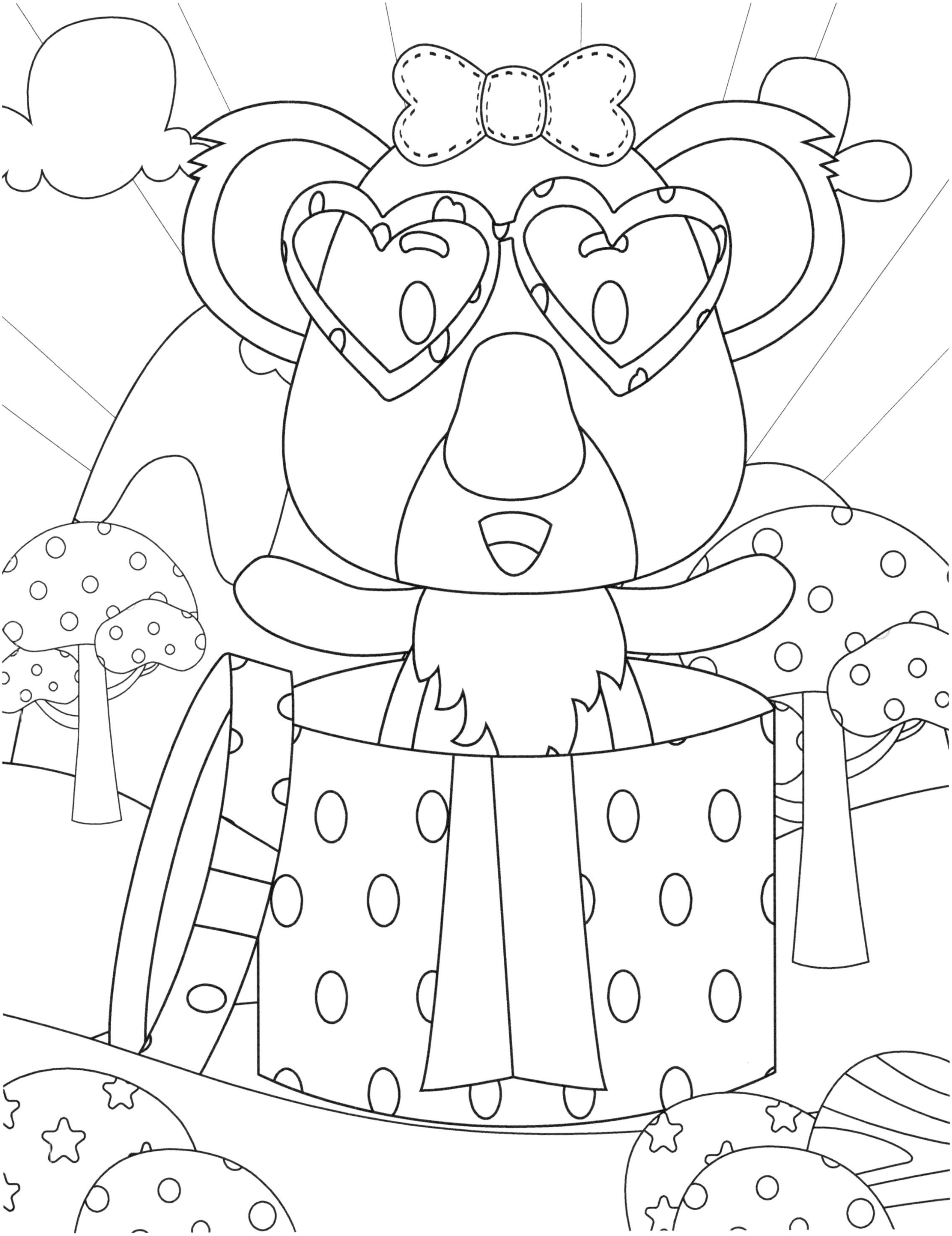

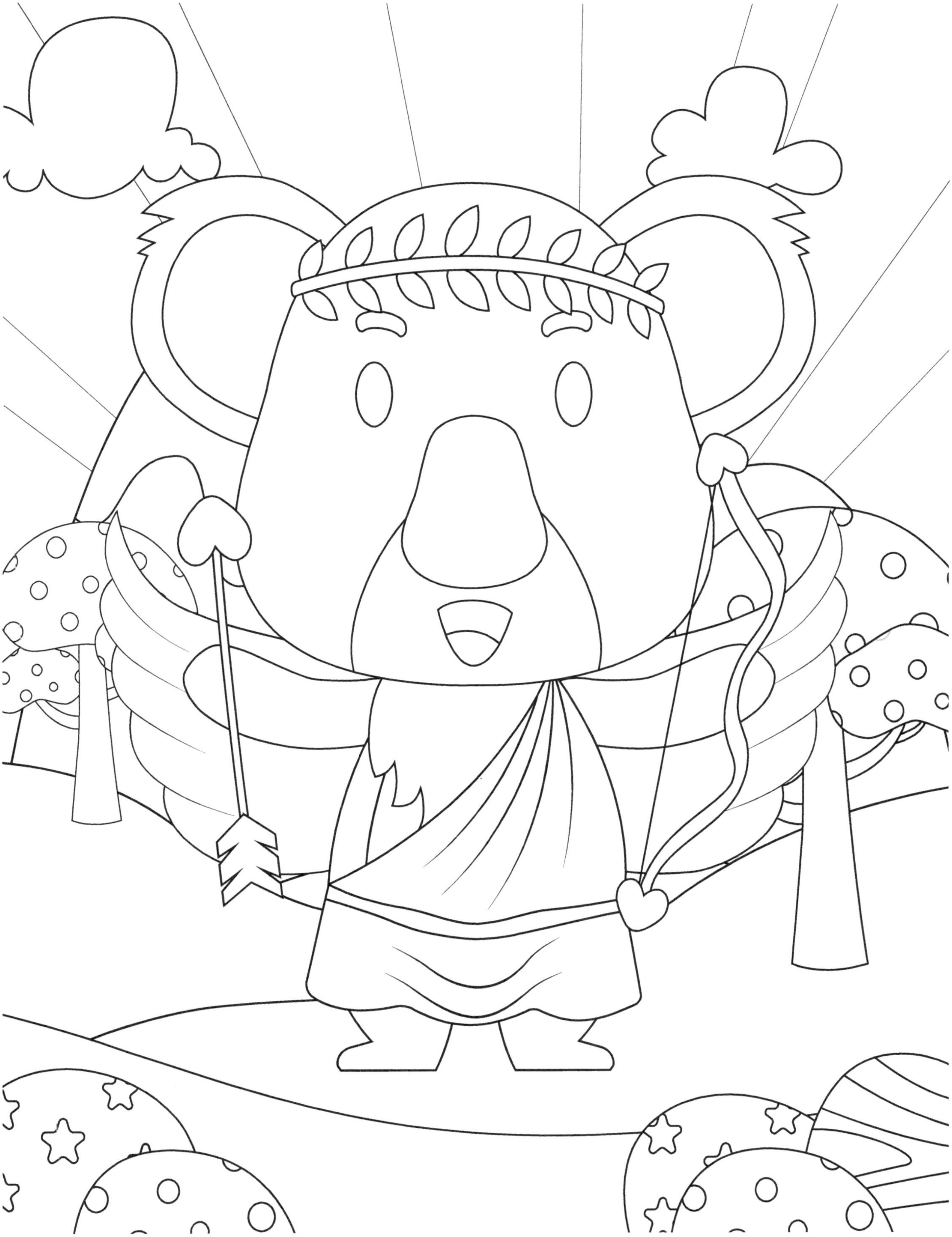

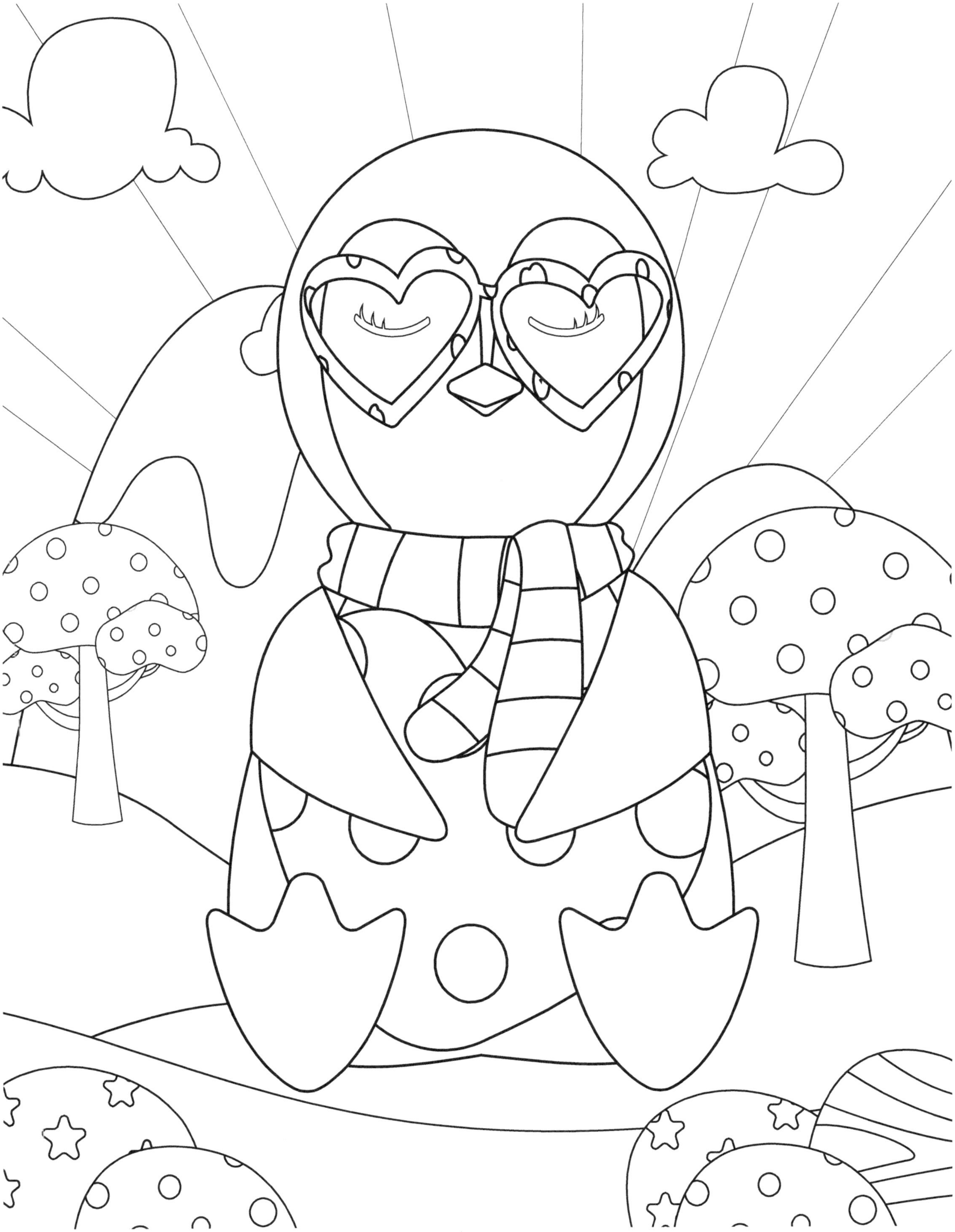

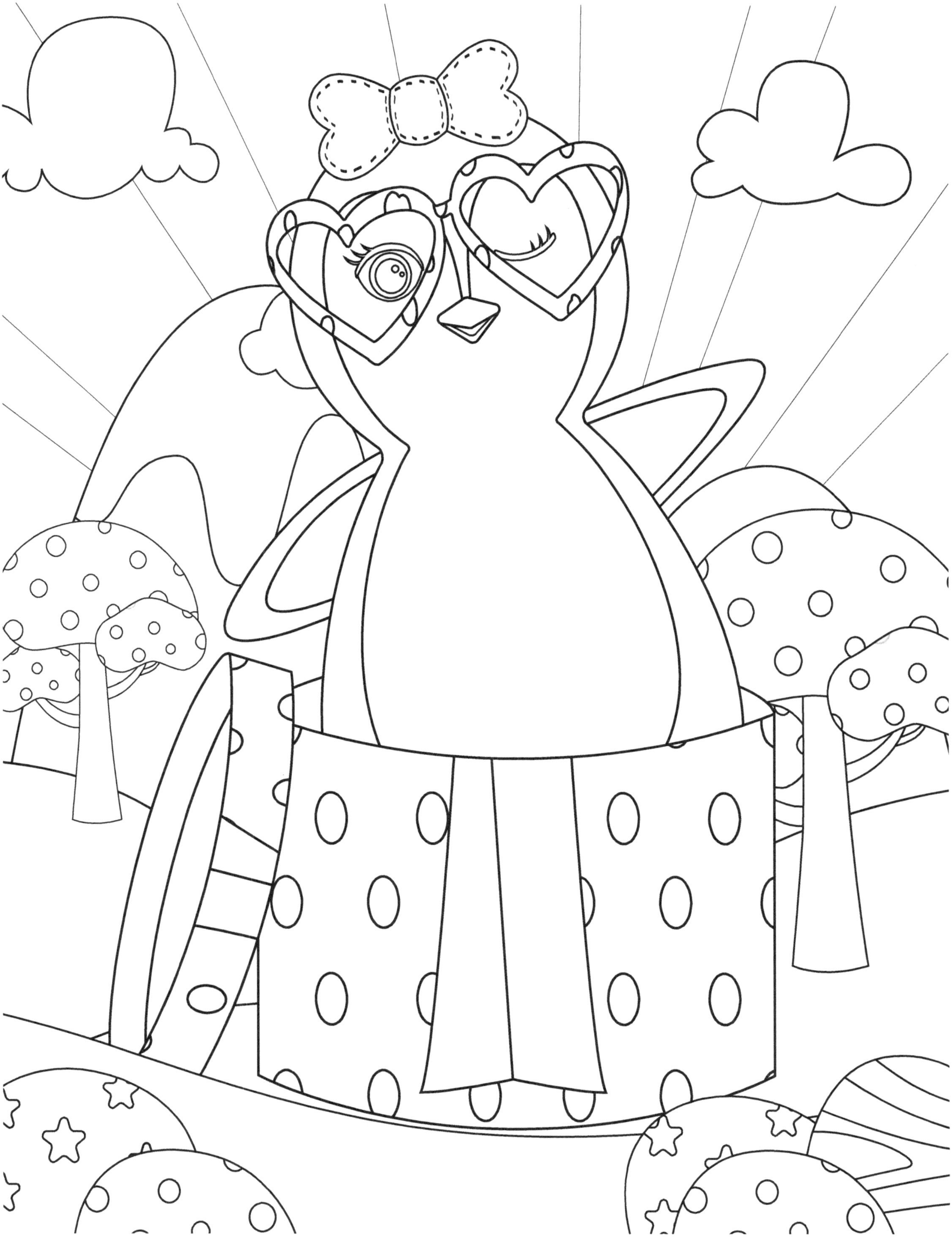

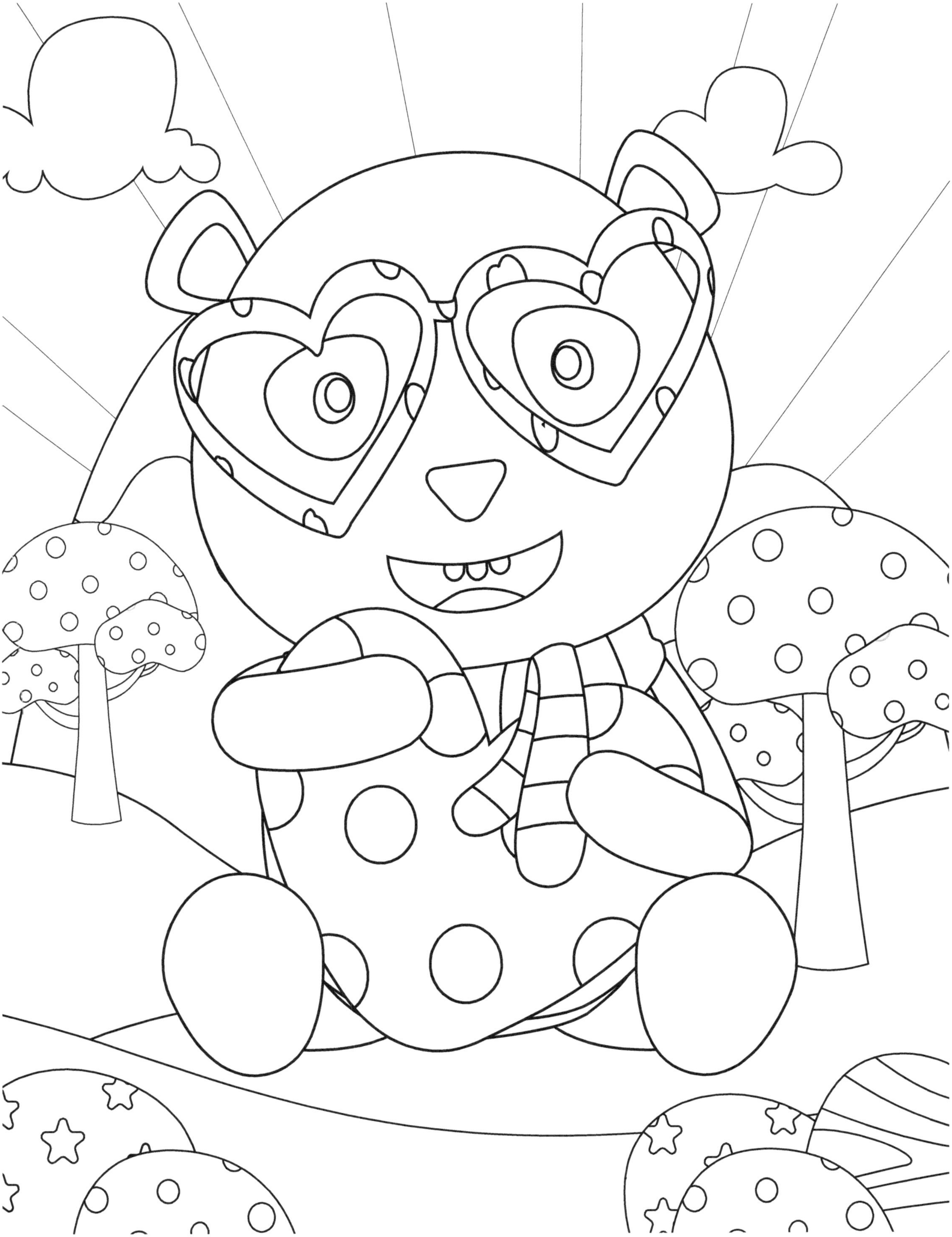

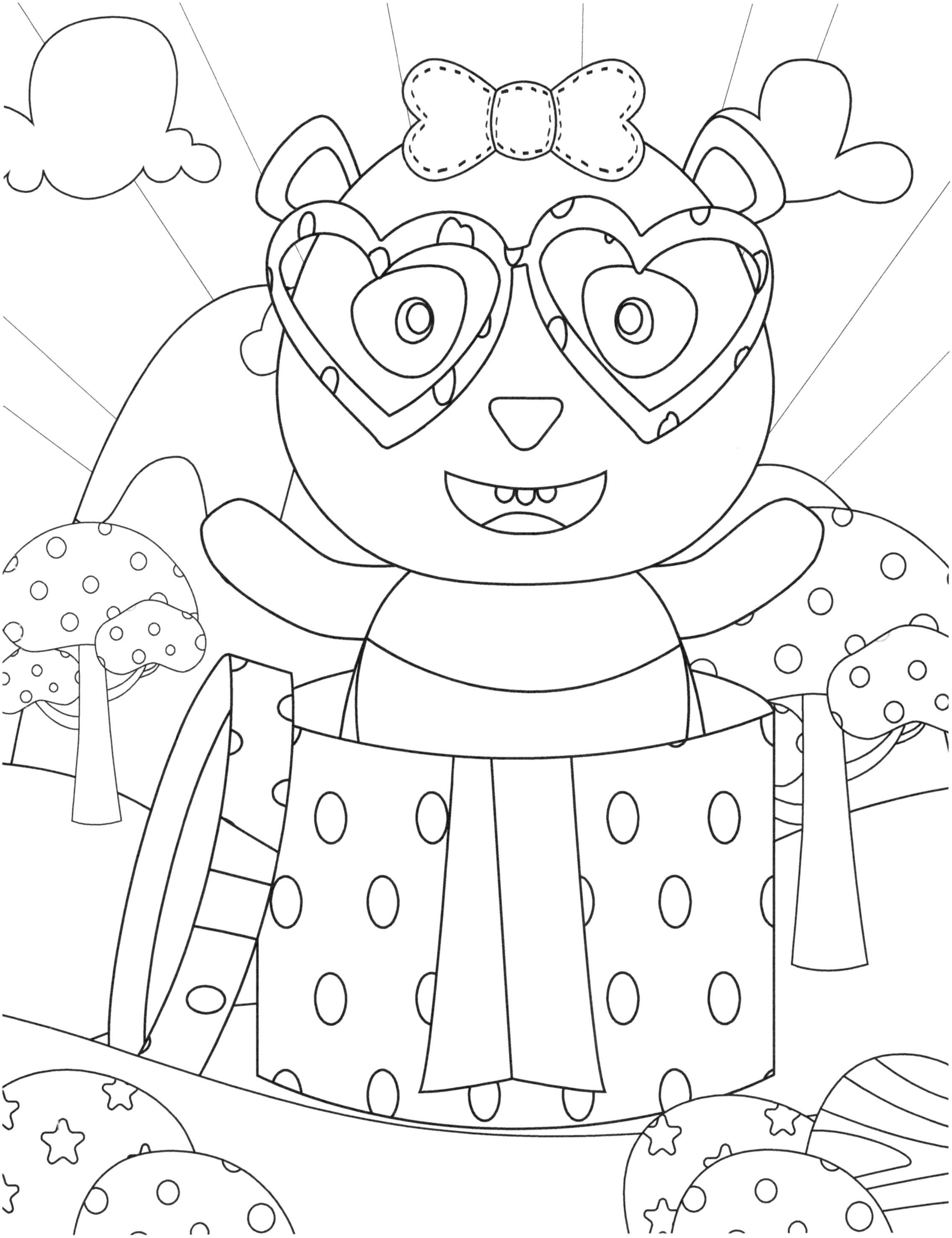

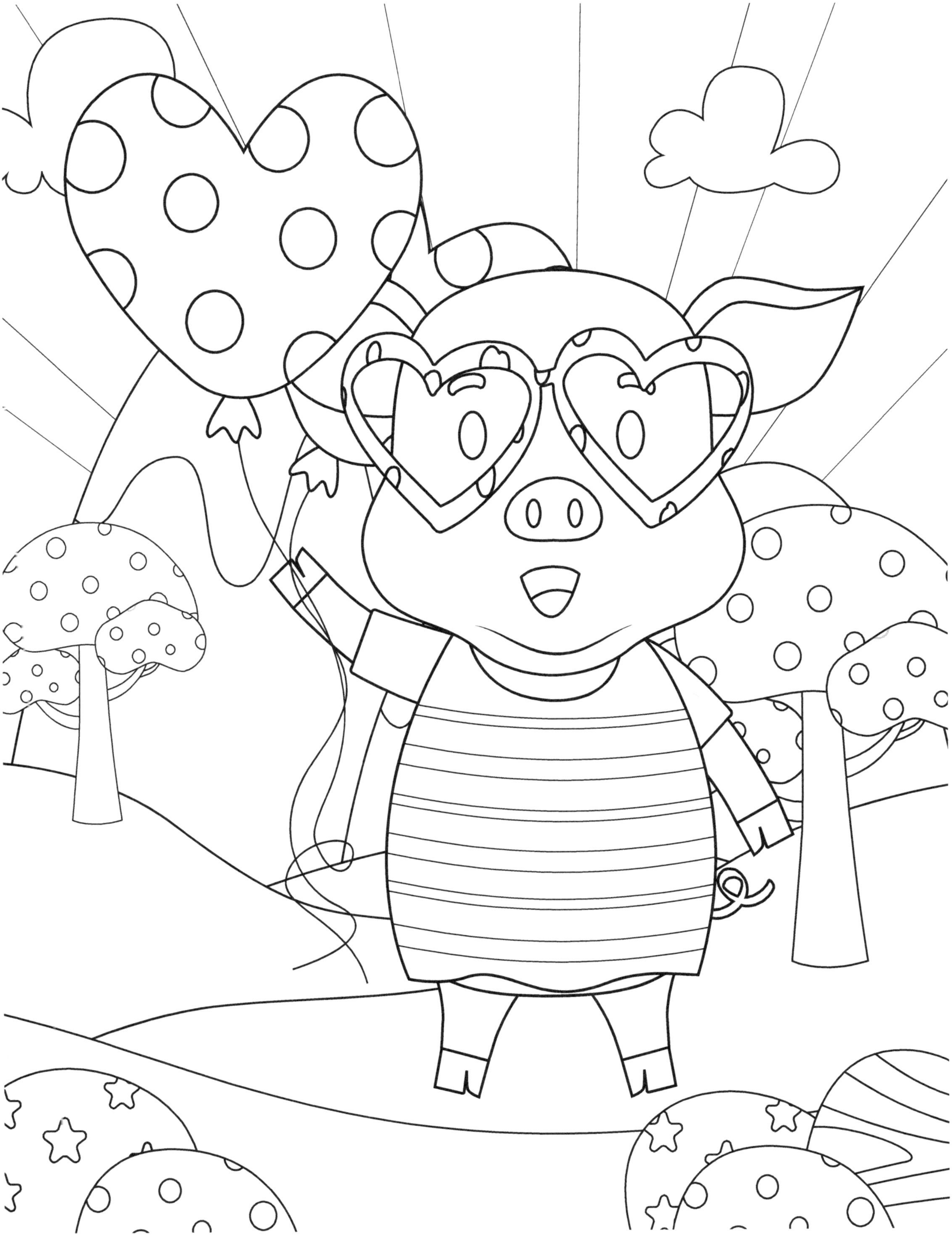

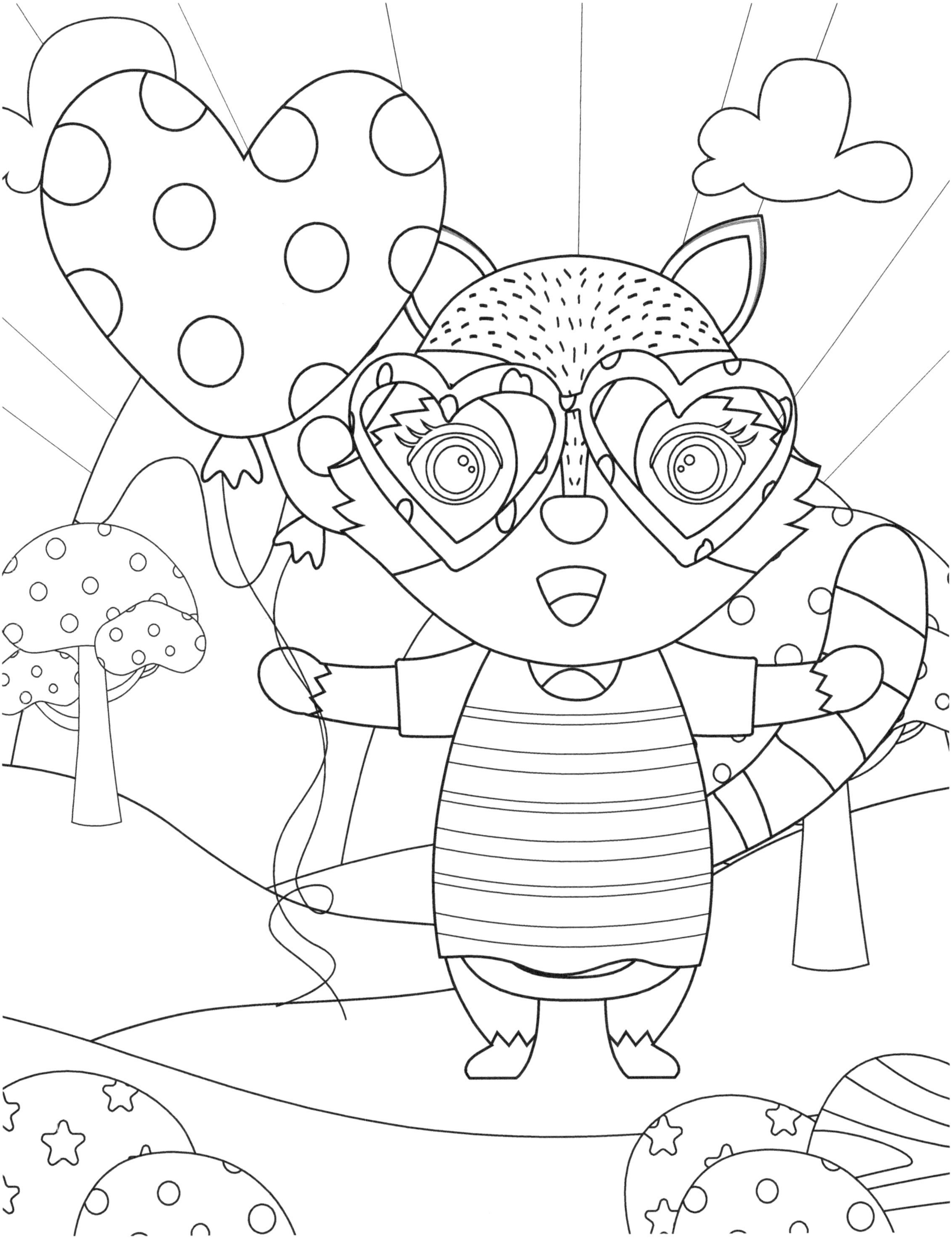

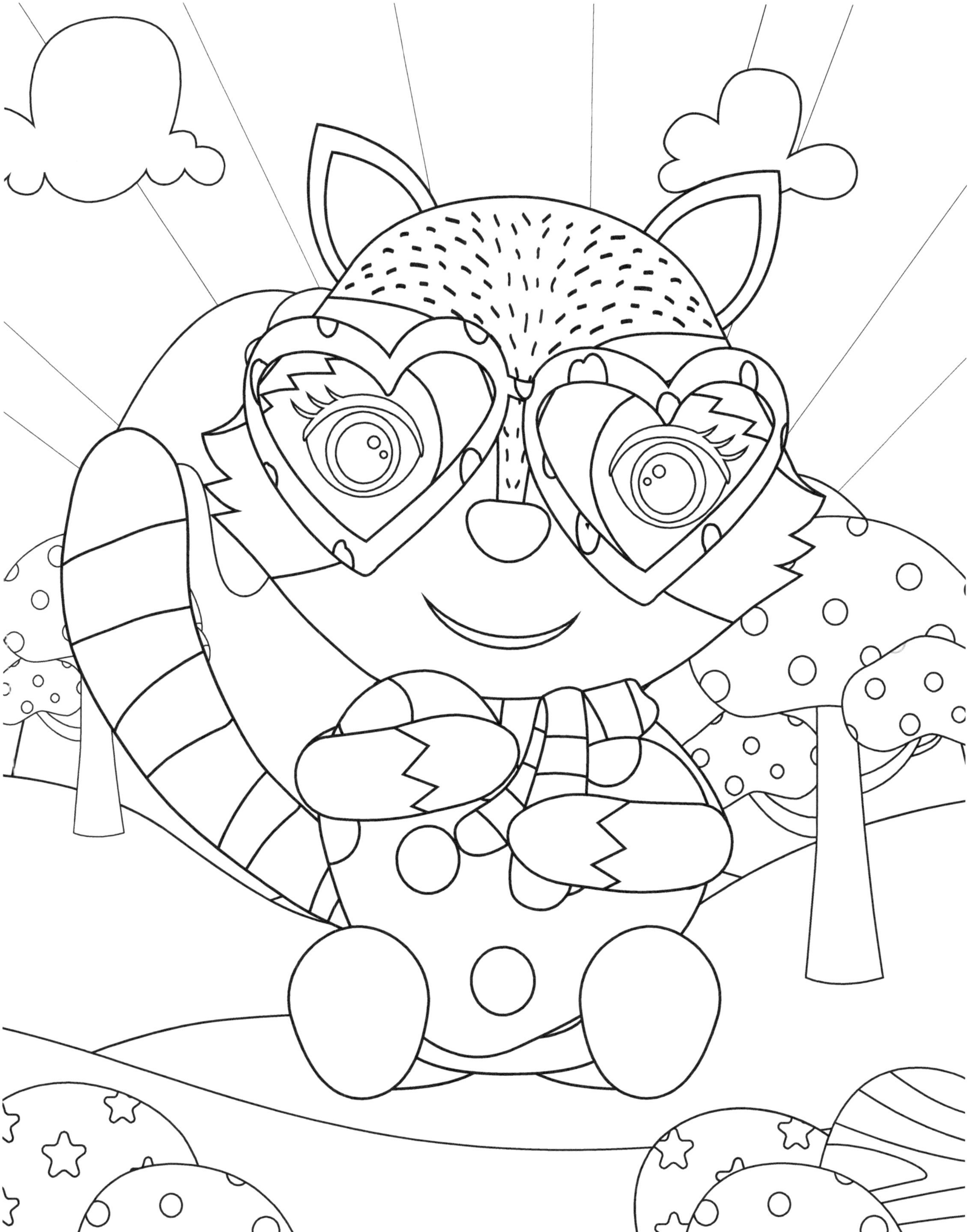

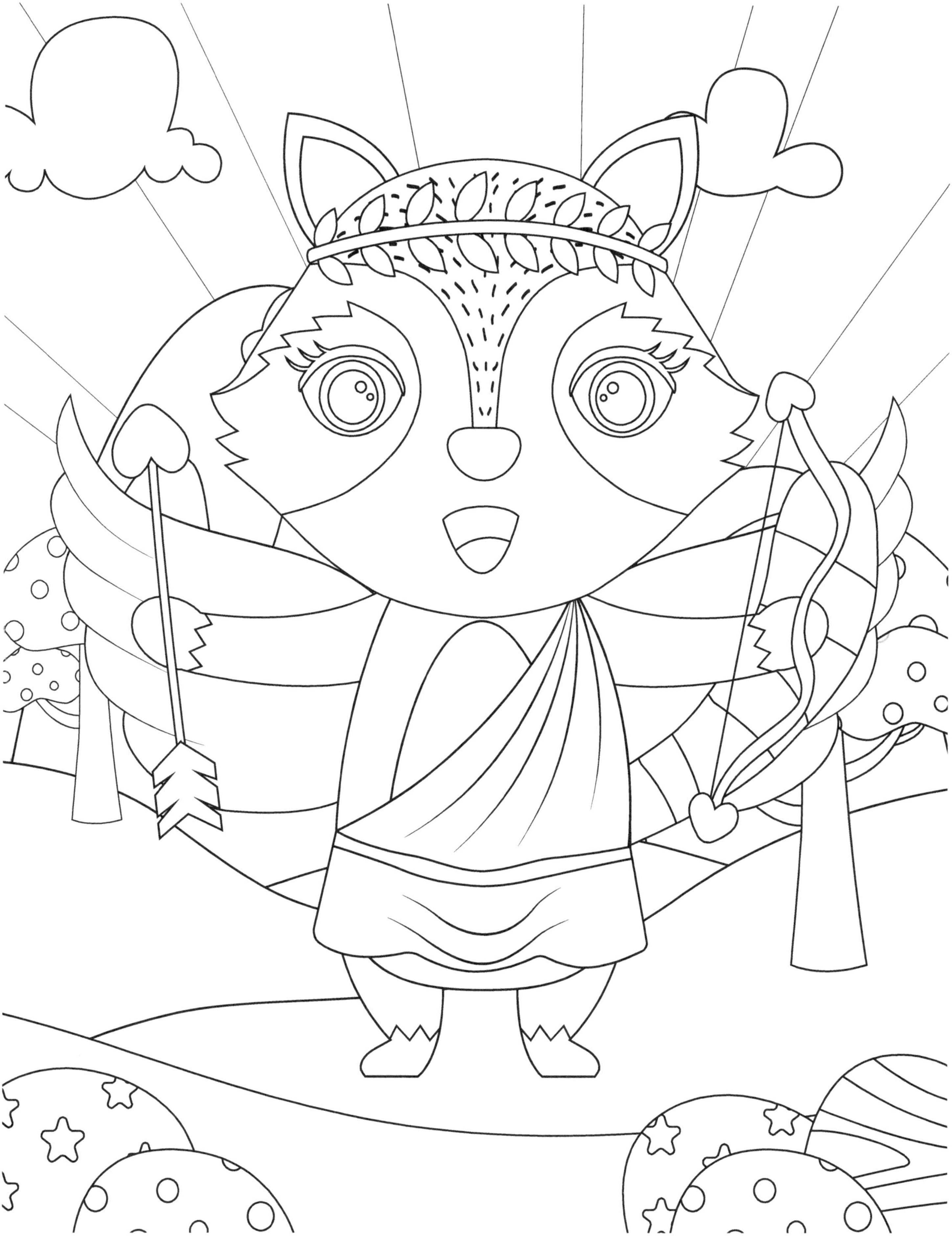

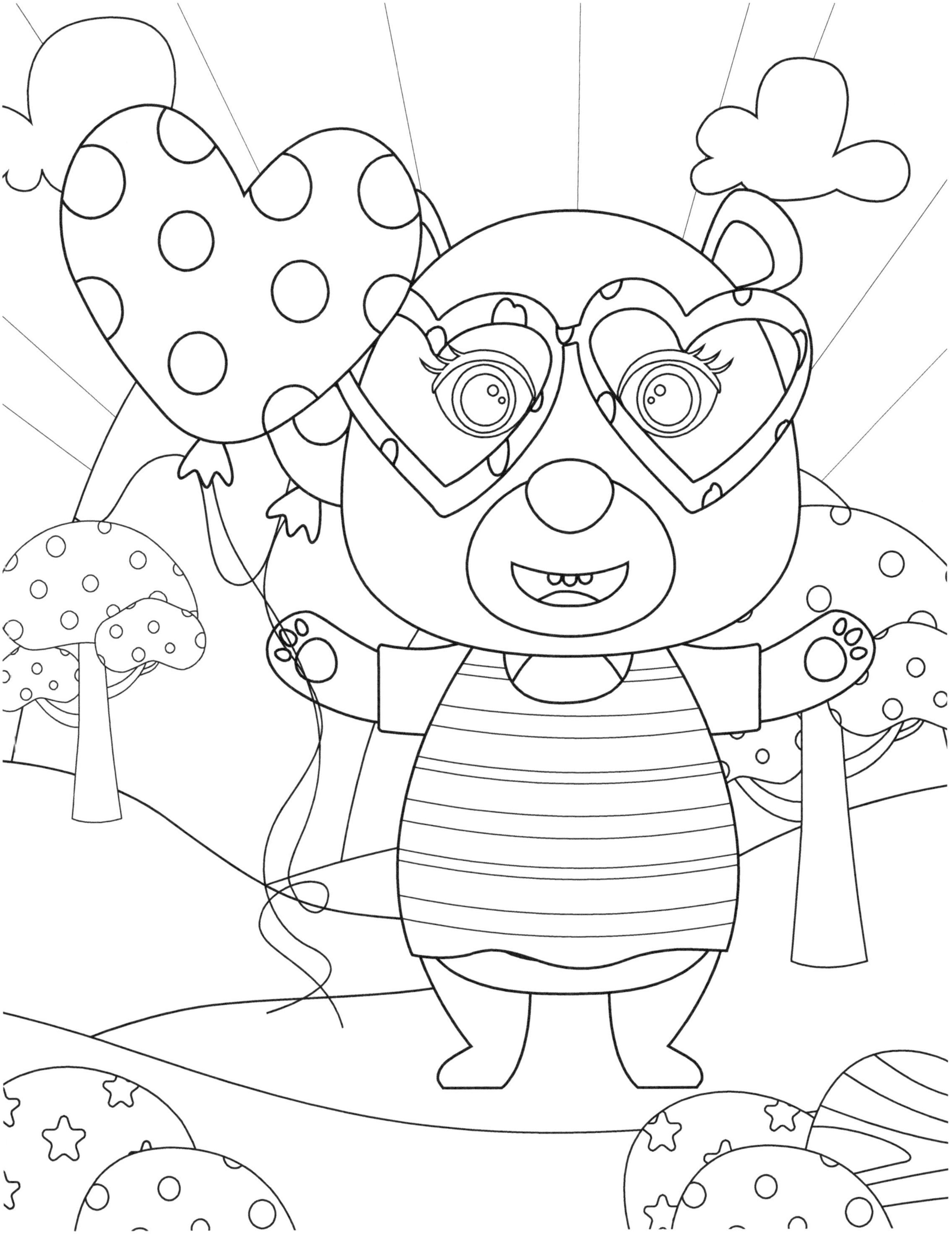

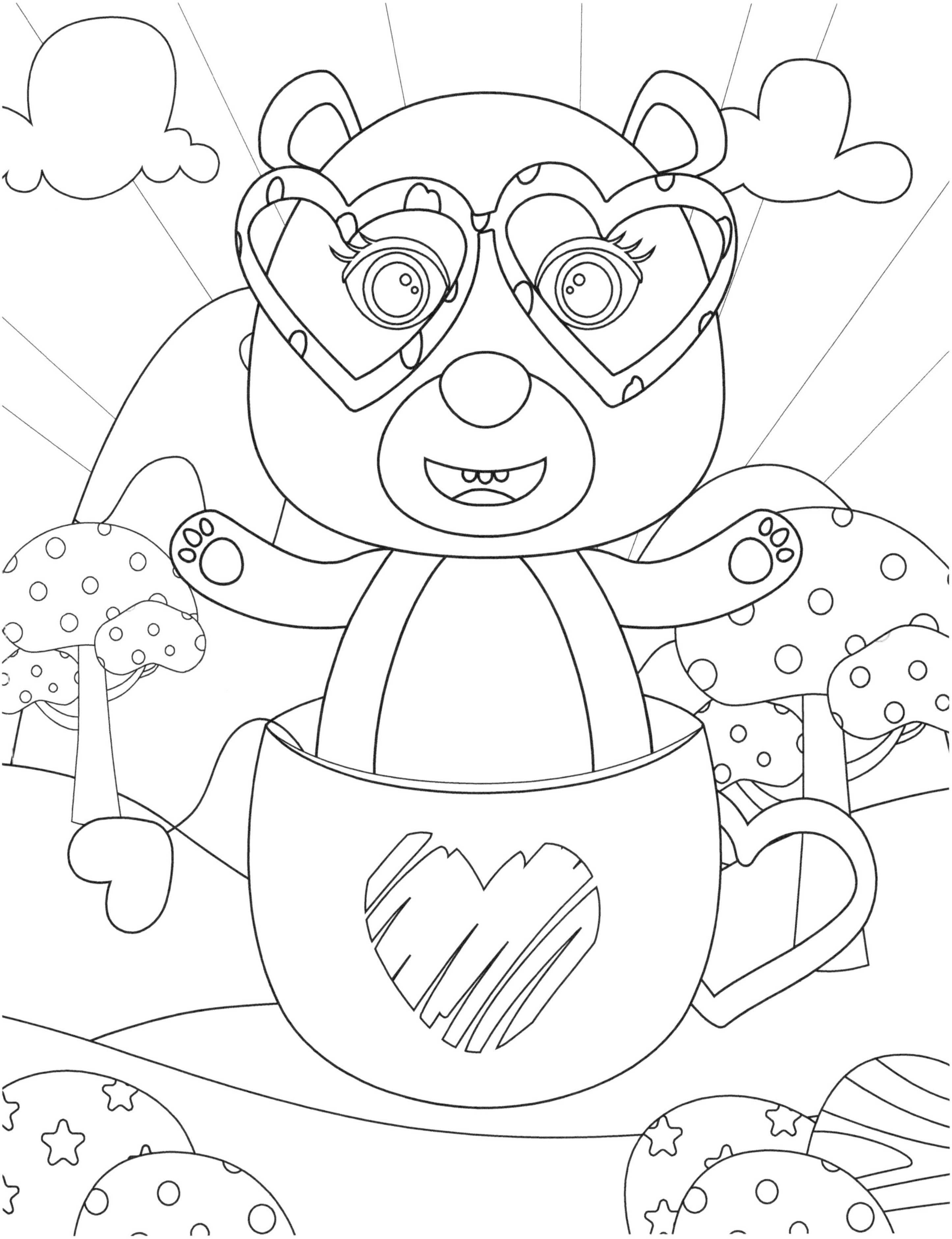

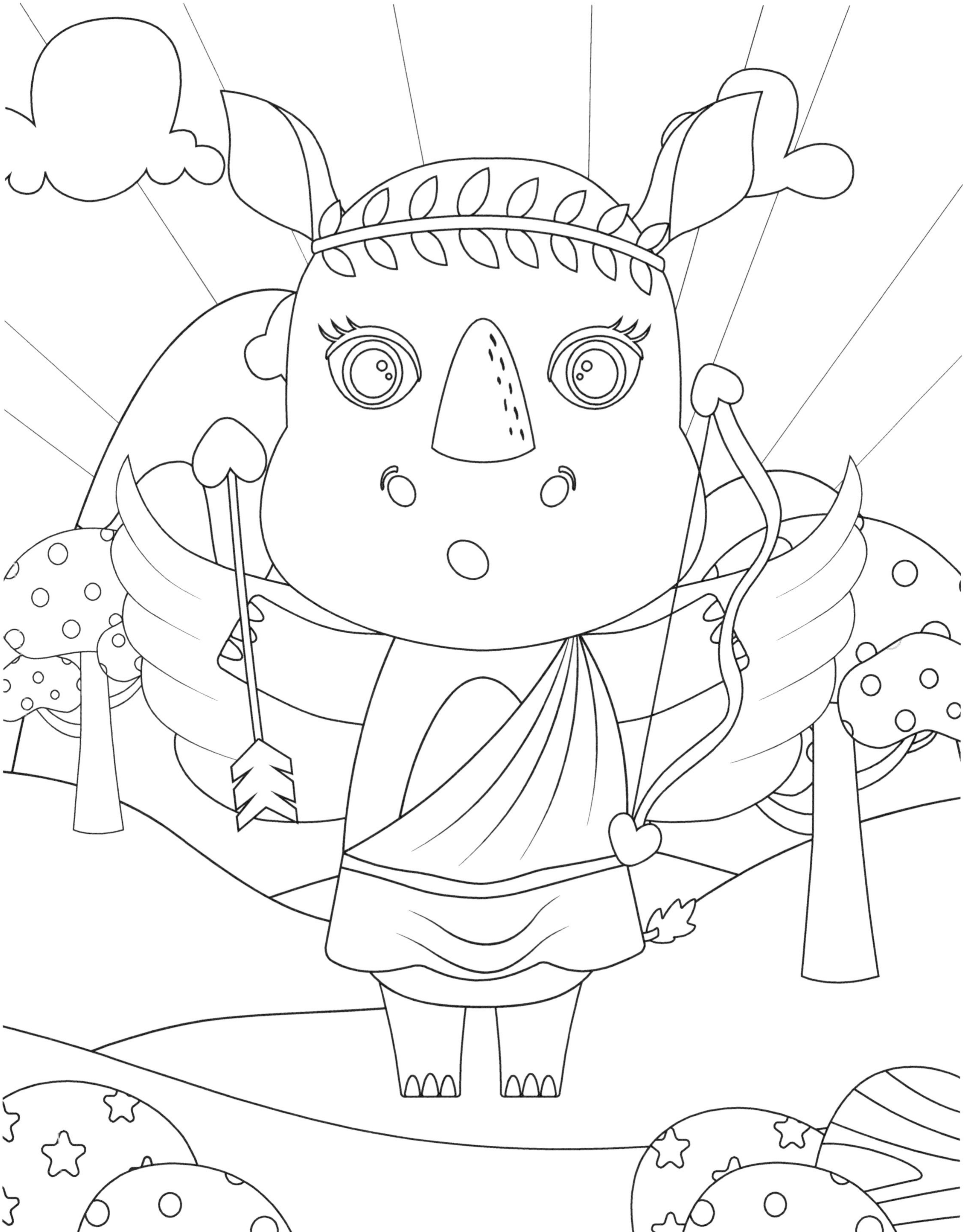

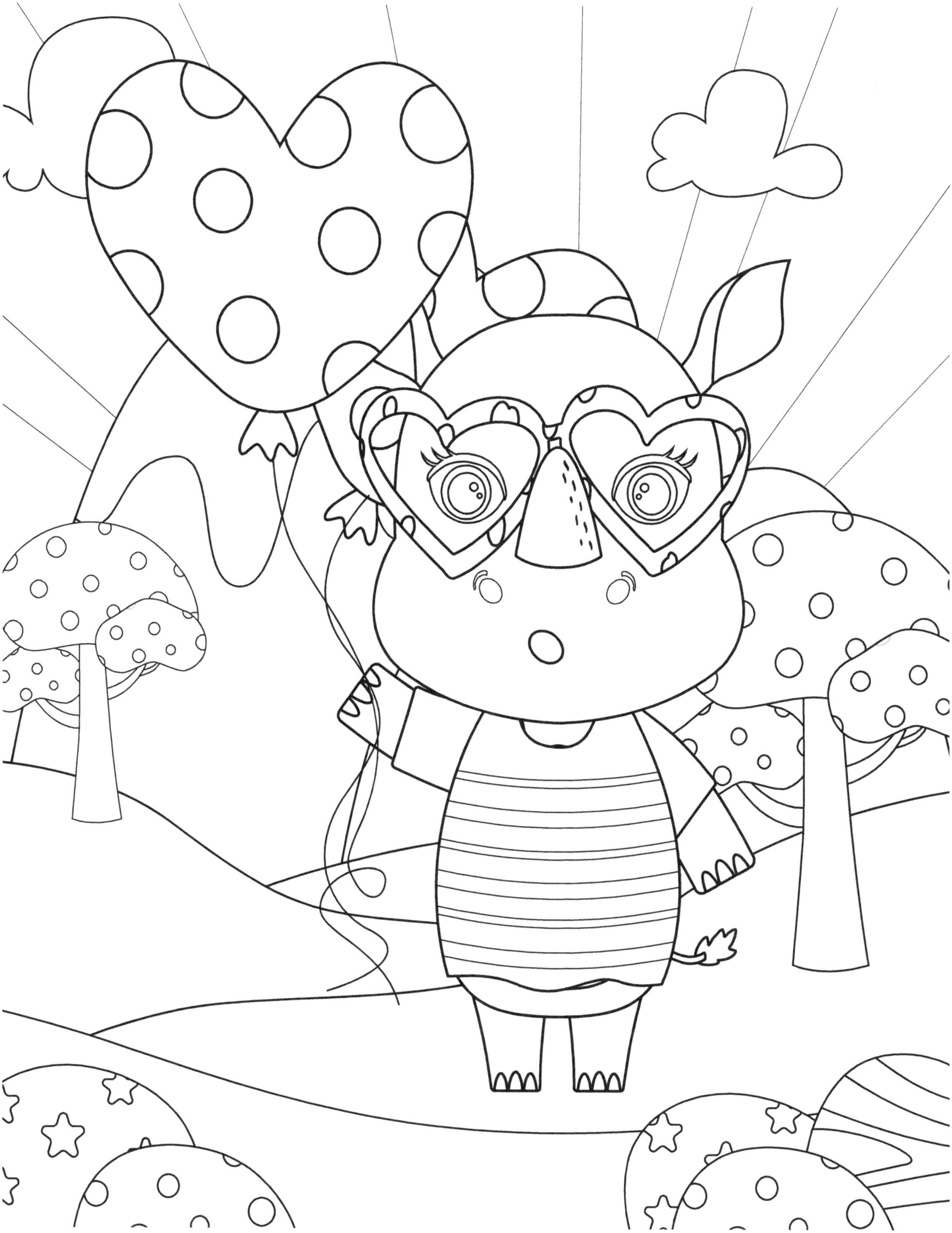

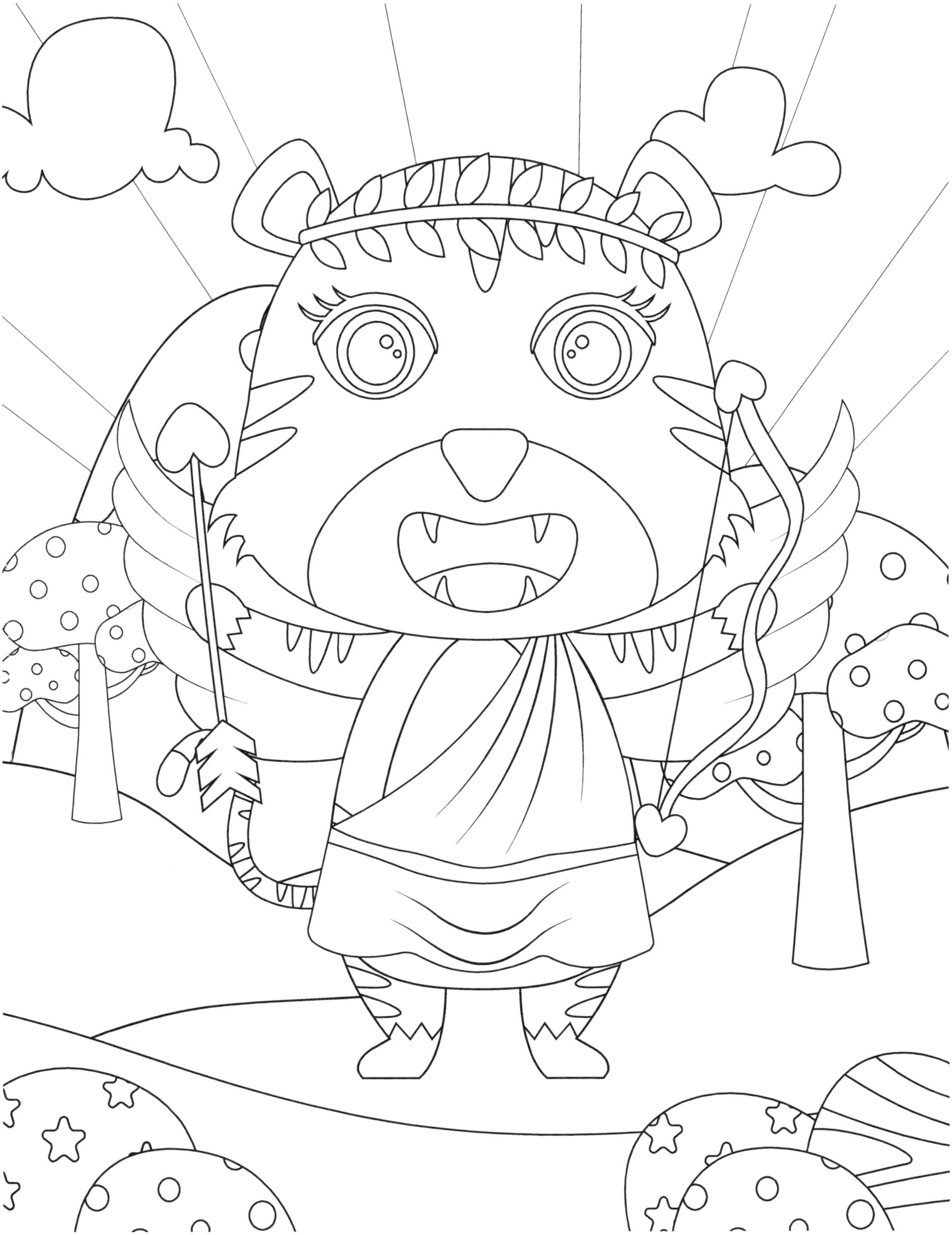

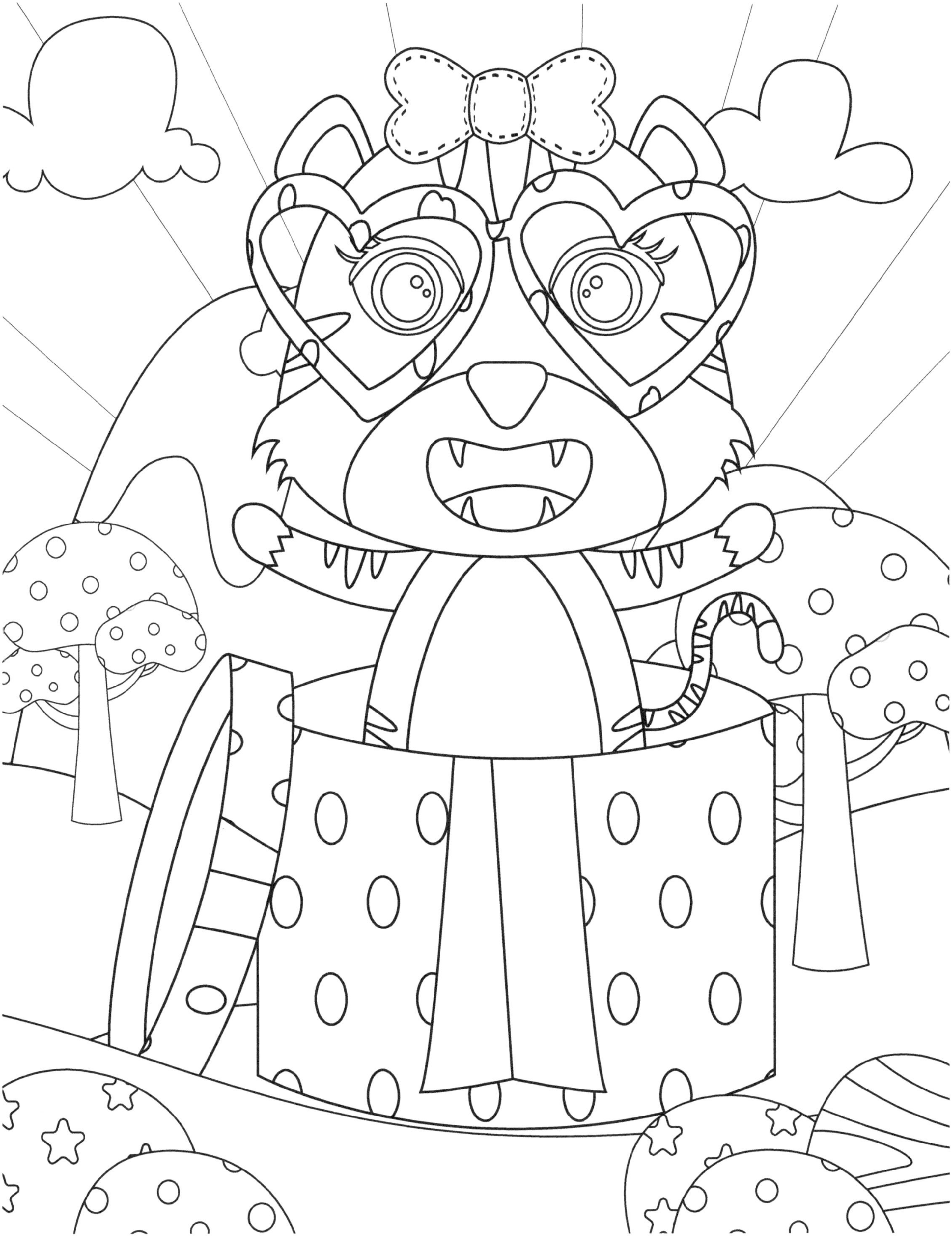

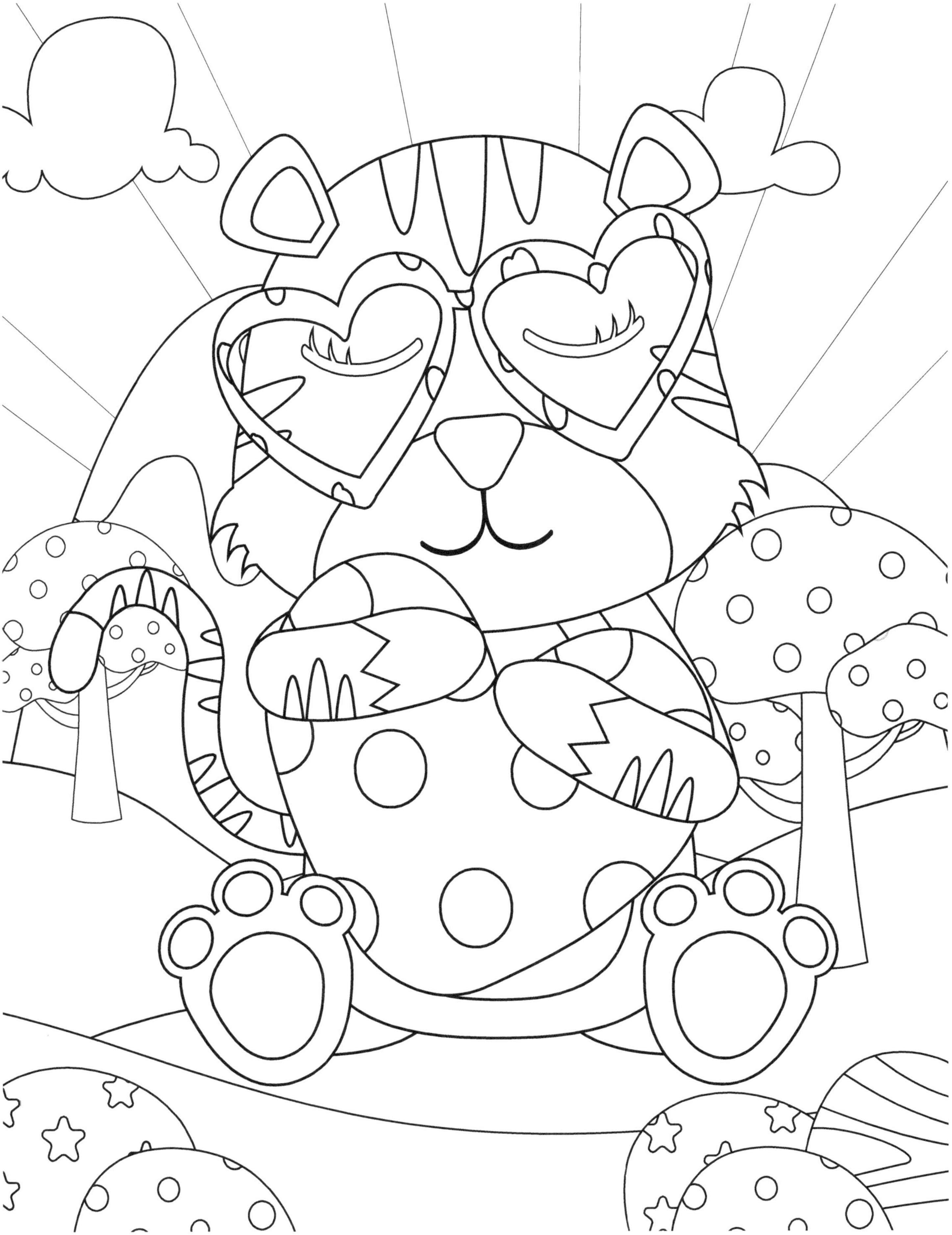

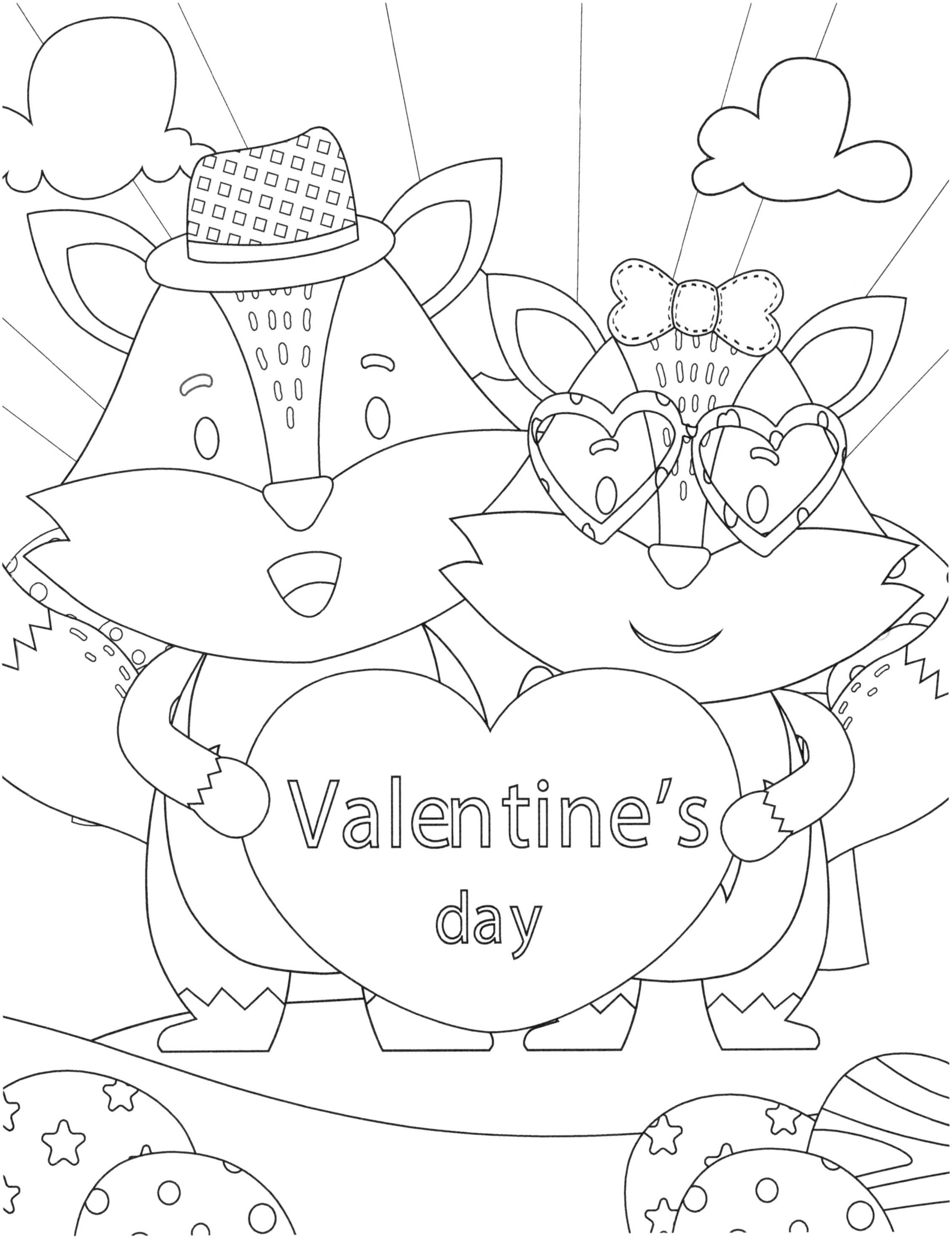
Valentine's
day

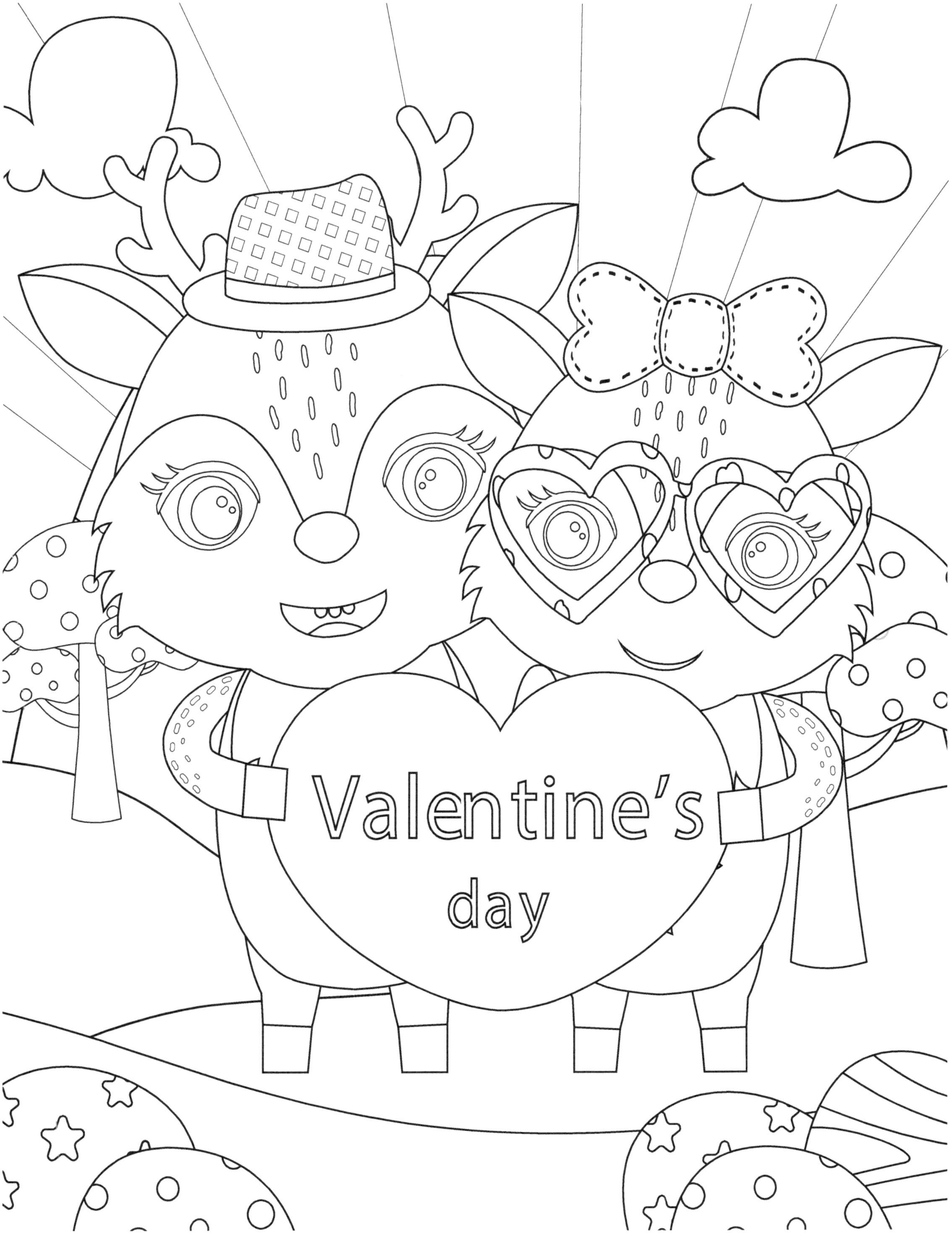
Valentine's
day

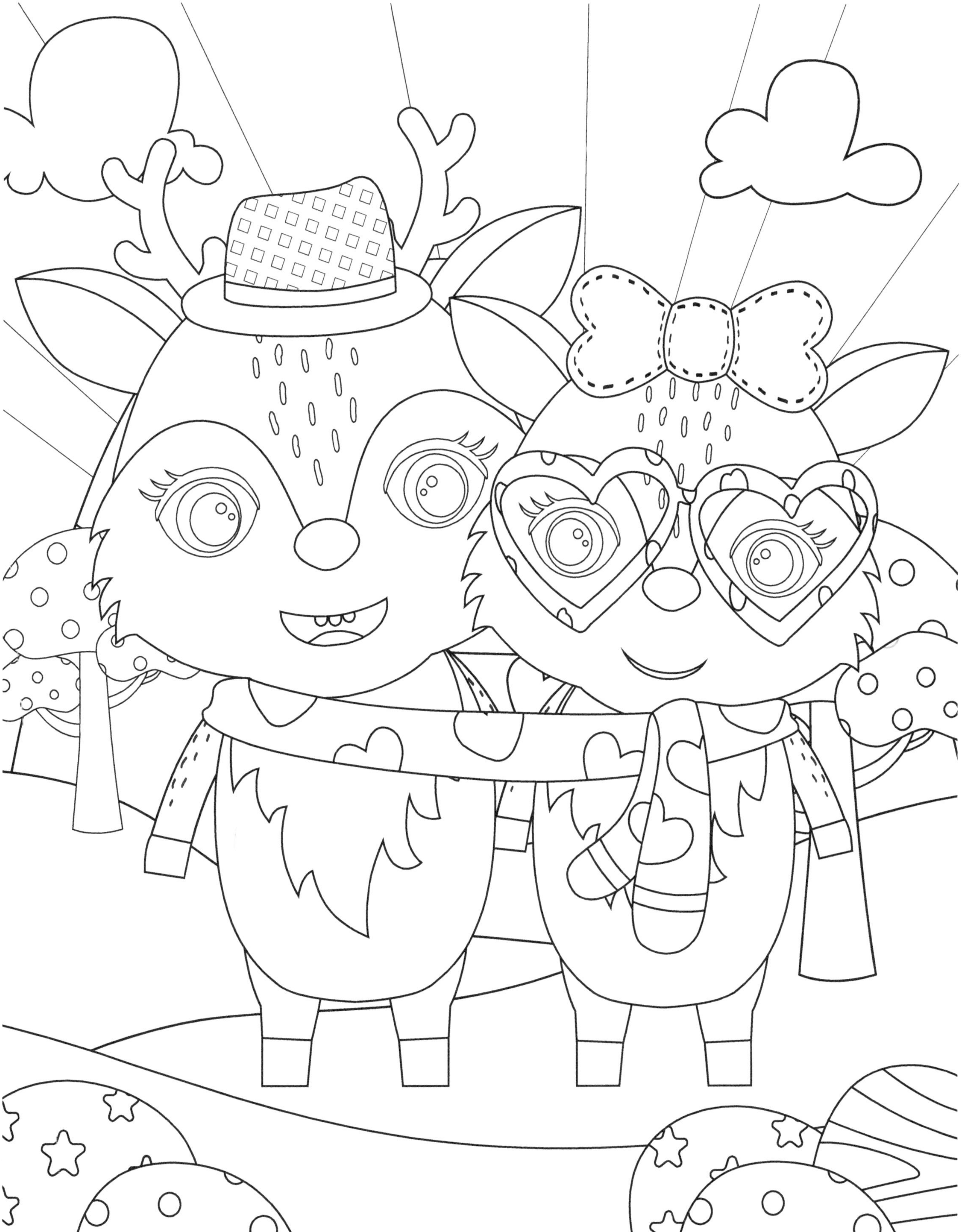

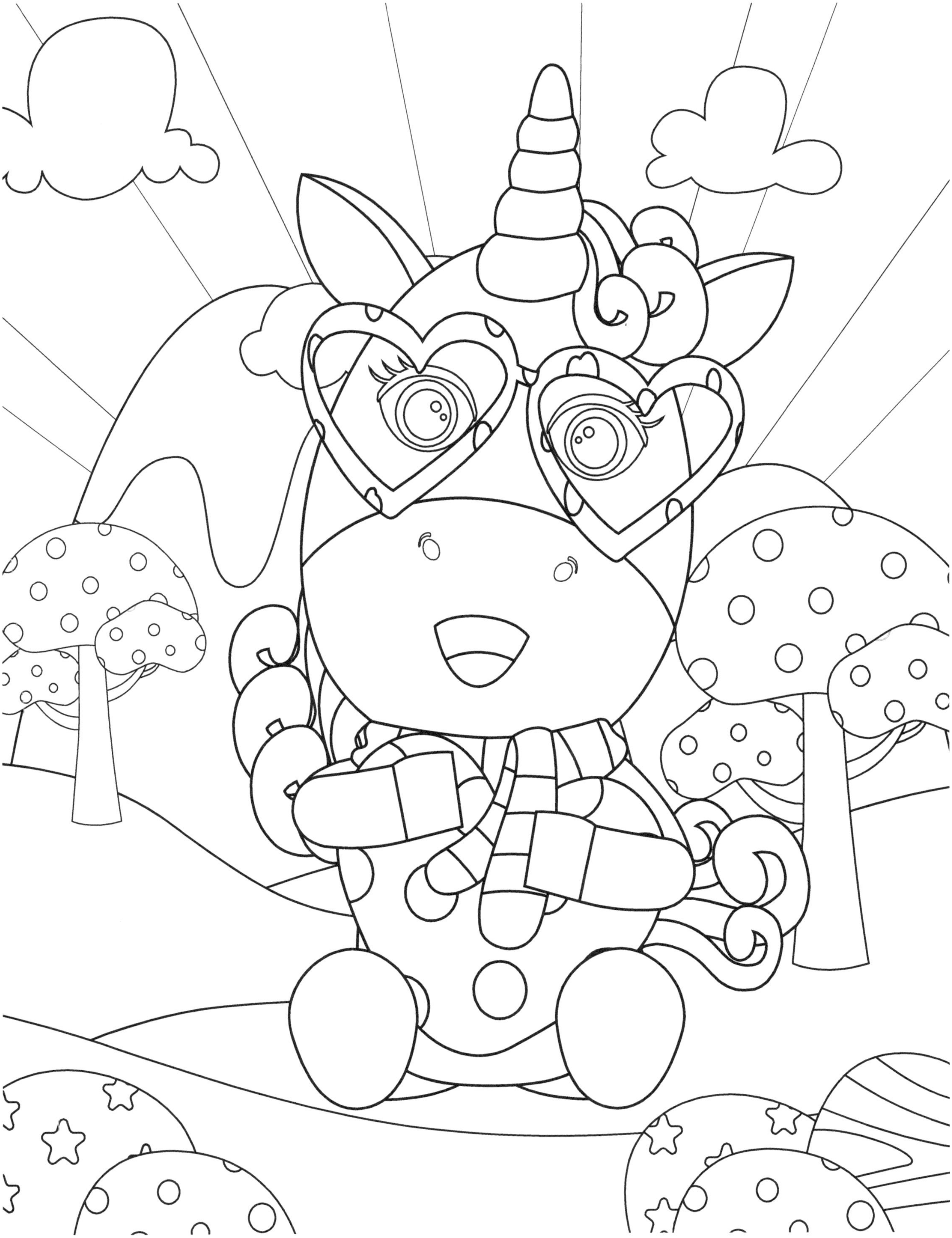

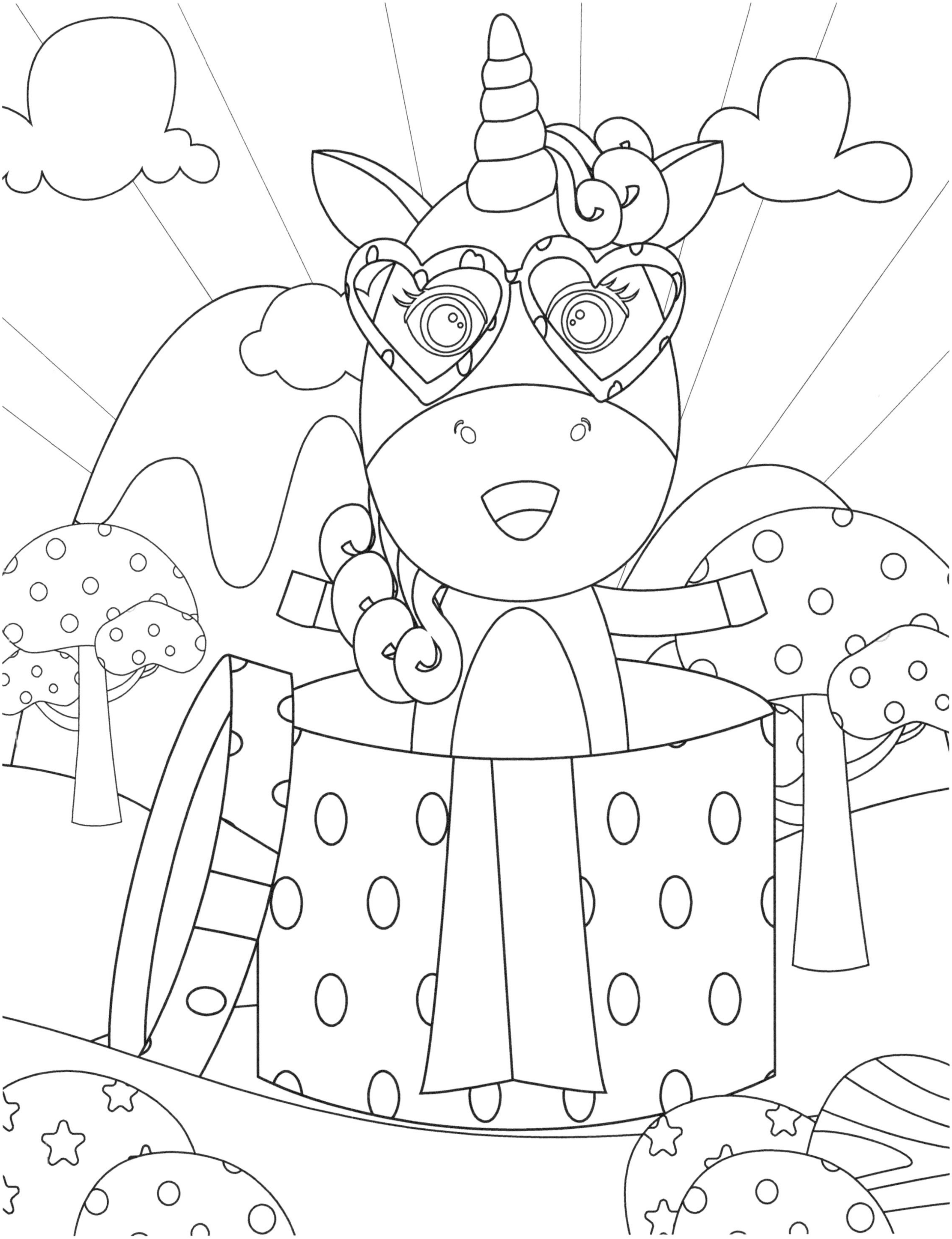

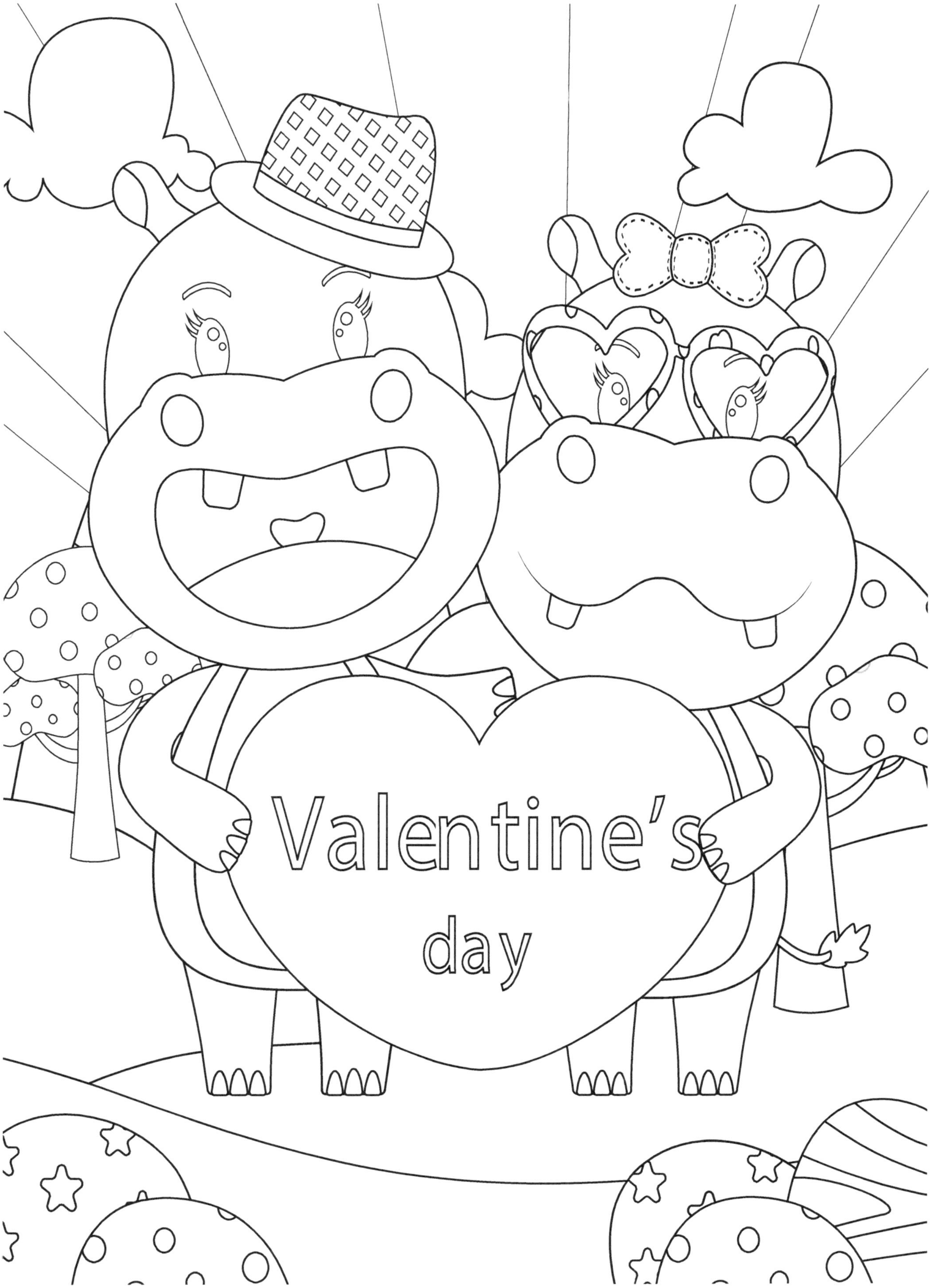
Valentine's
day

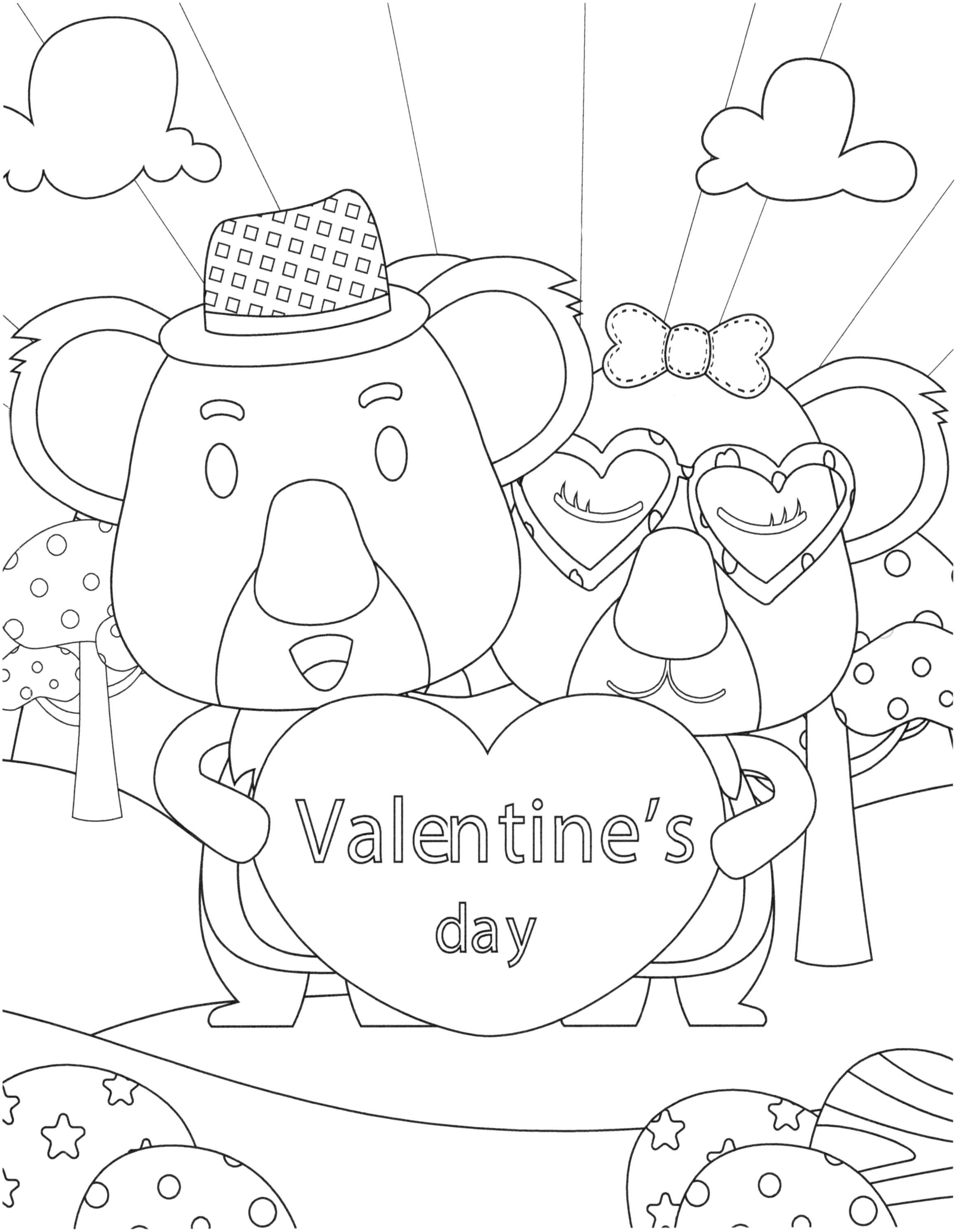
Valentine's
day

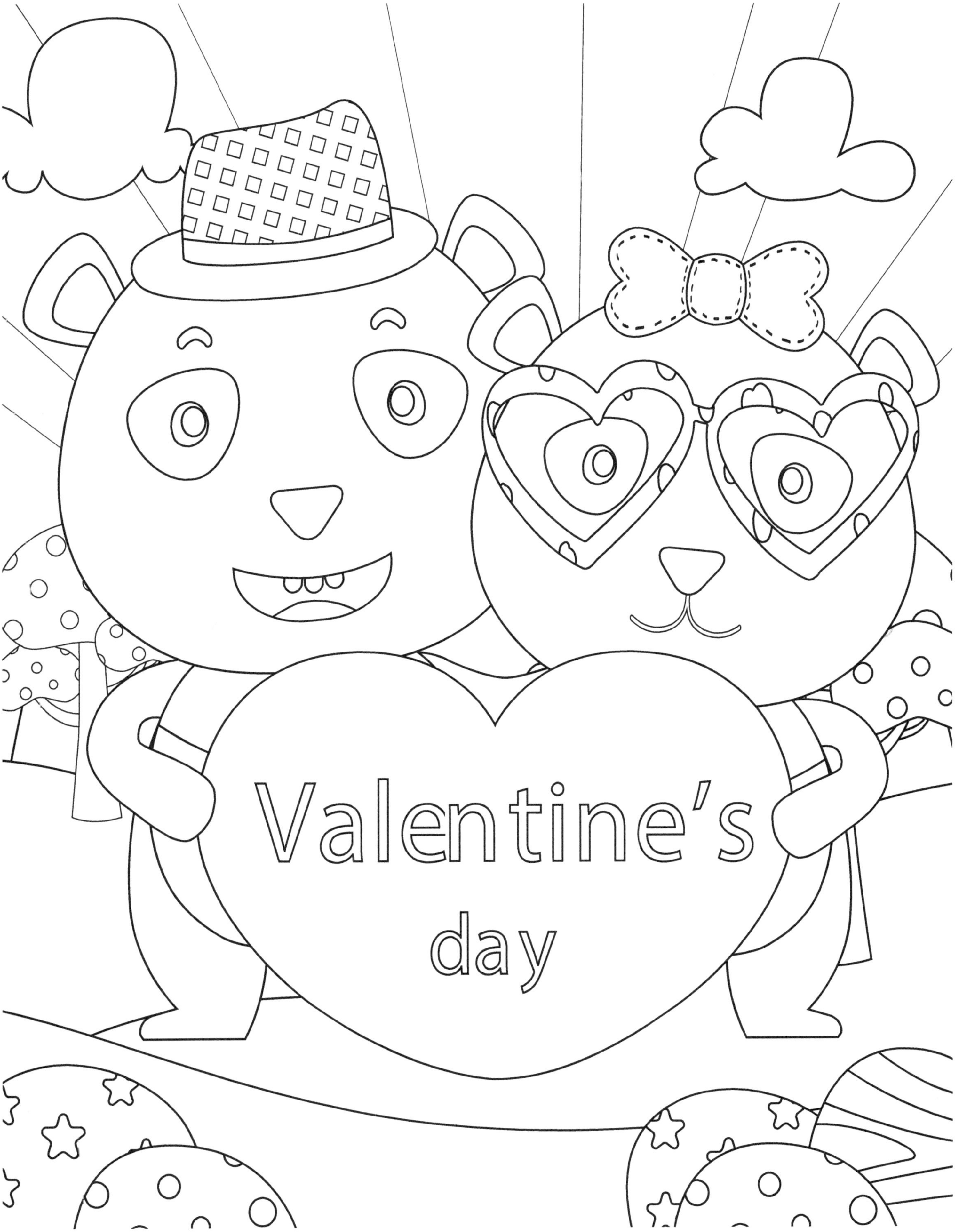
Valentine's
day

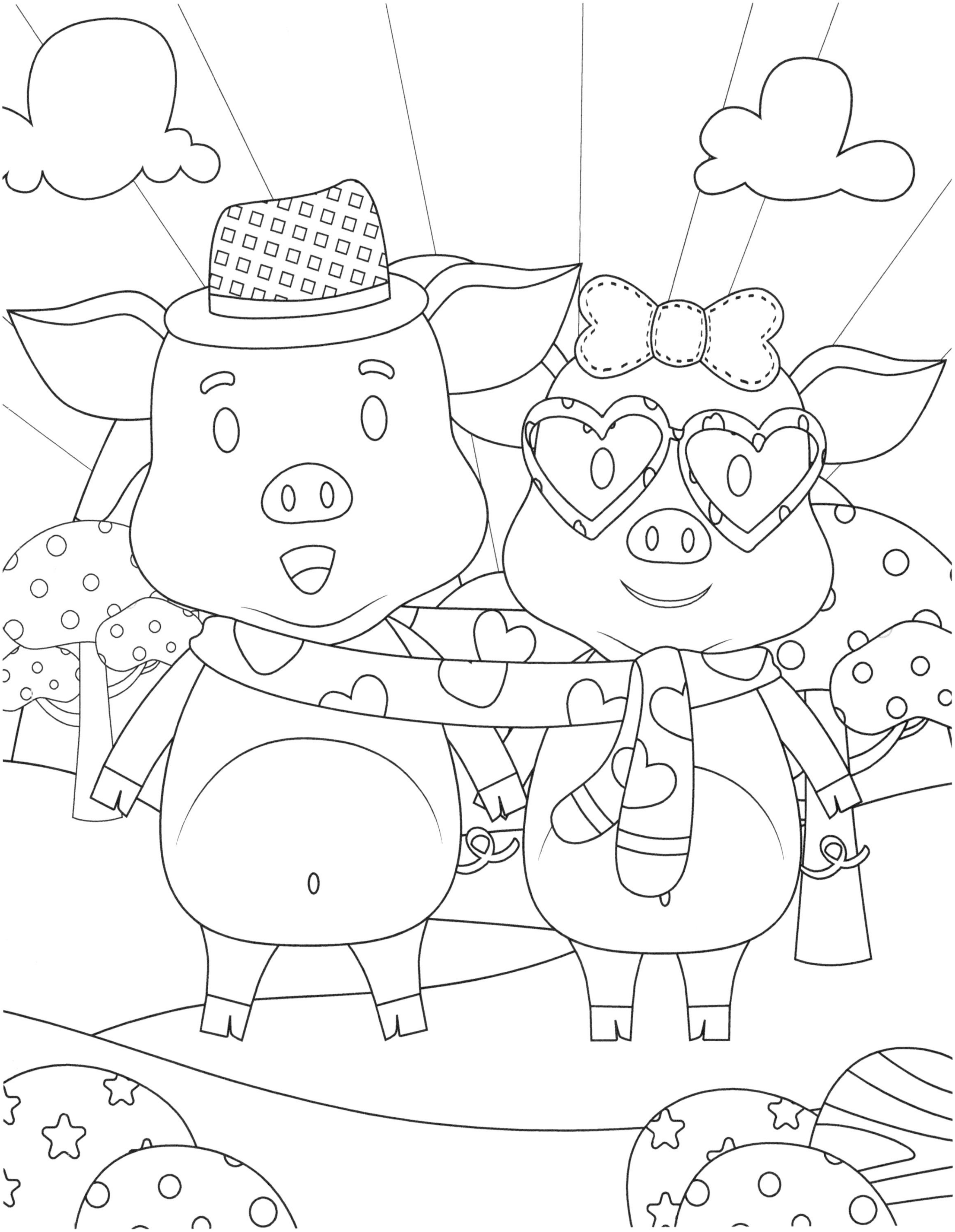

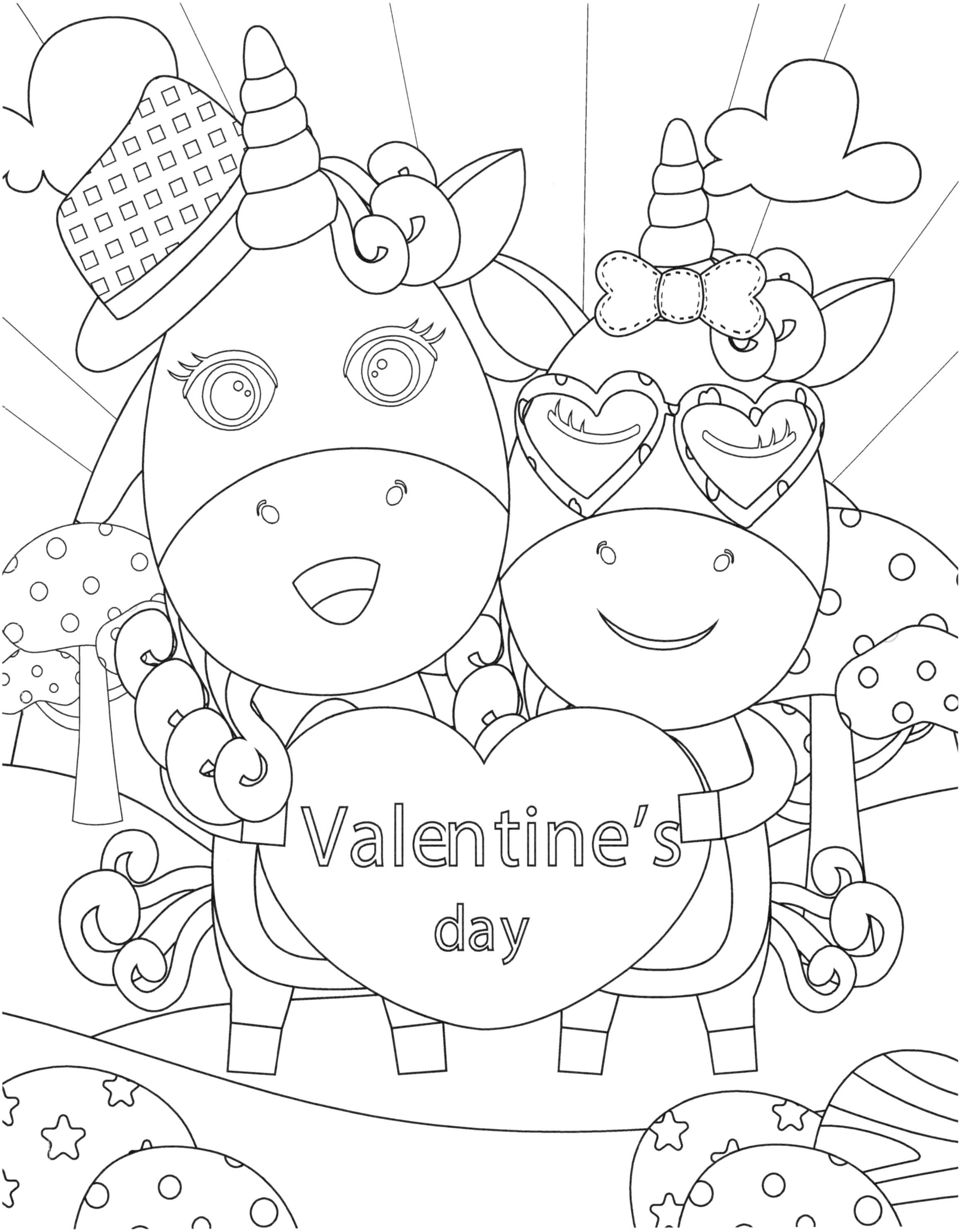
Valentine's
day

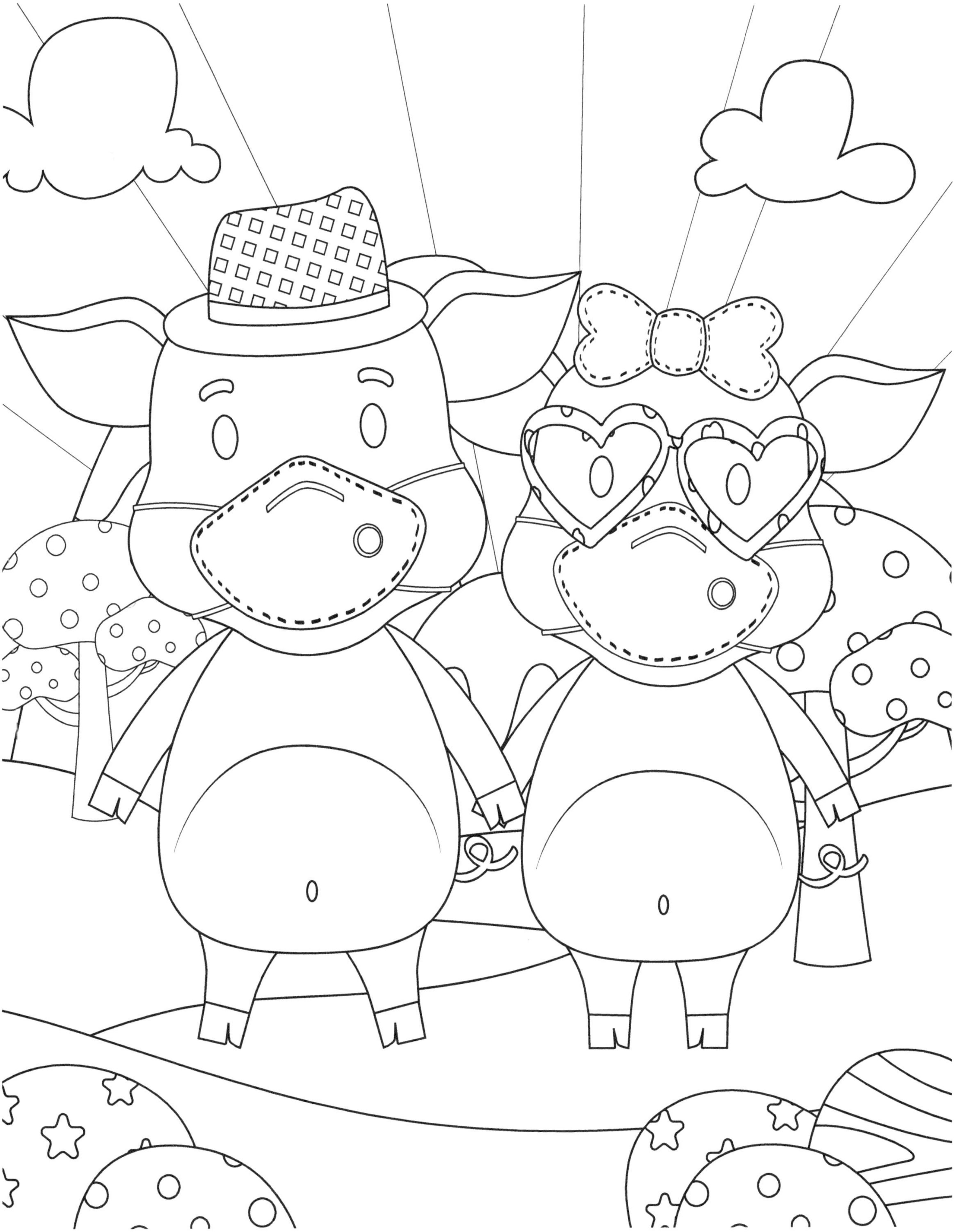

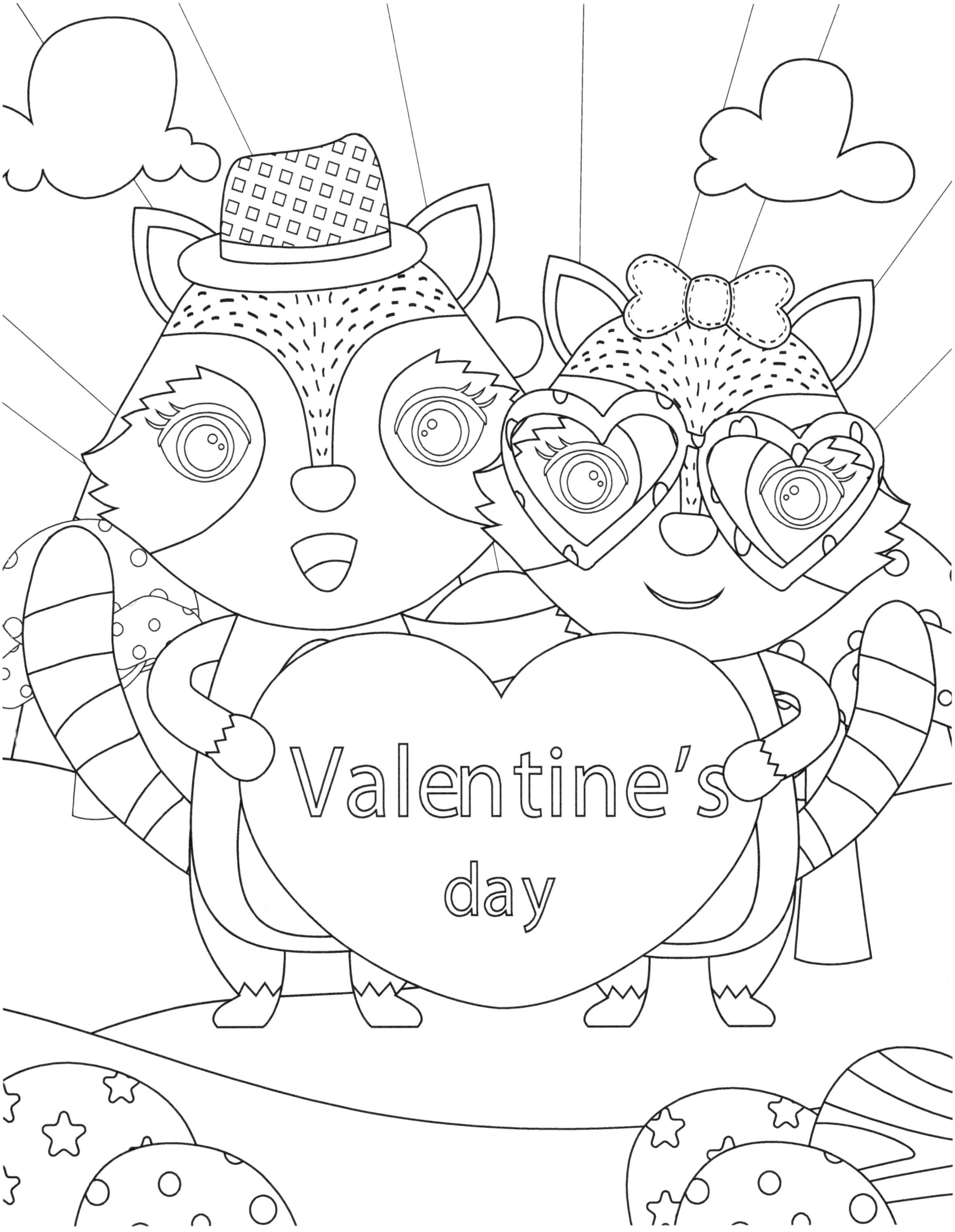
Valentine's
day

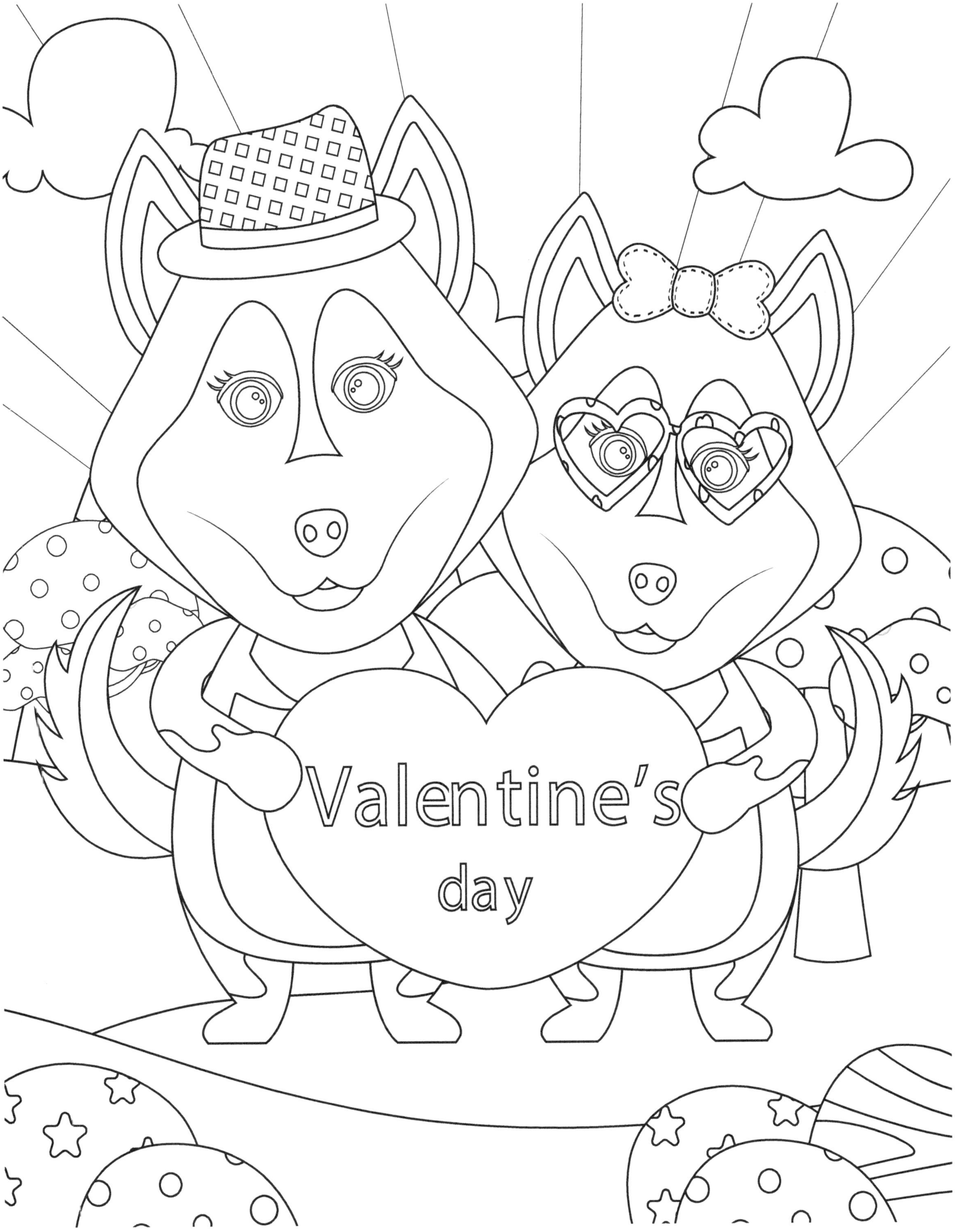
Valentine's
day

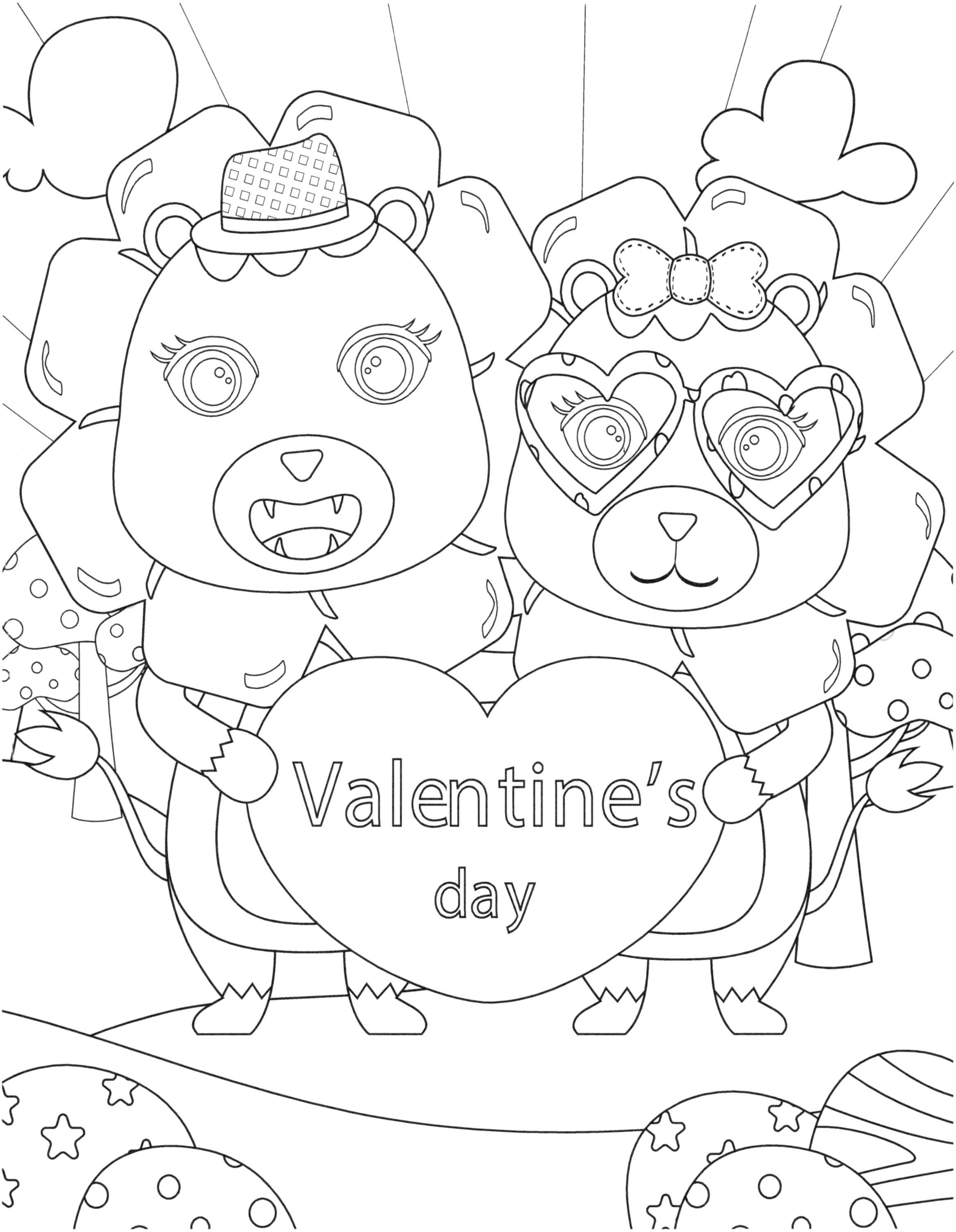
Valentine's
day

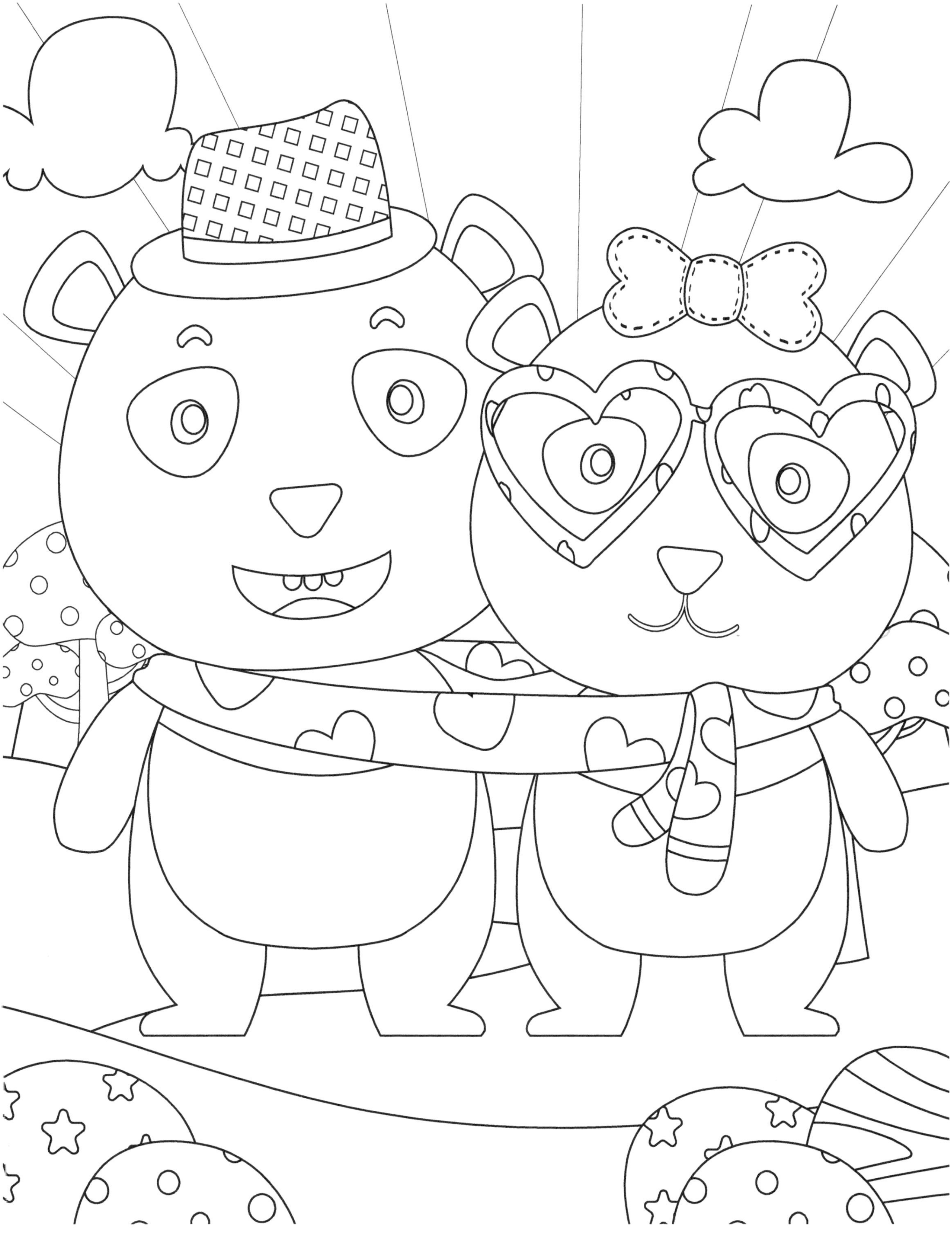

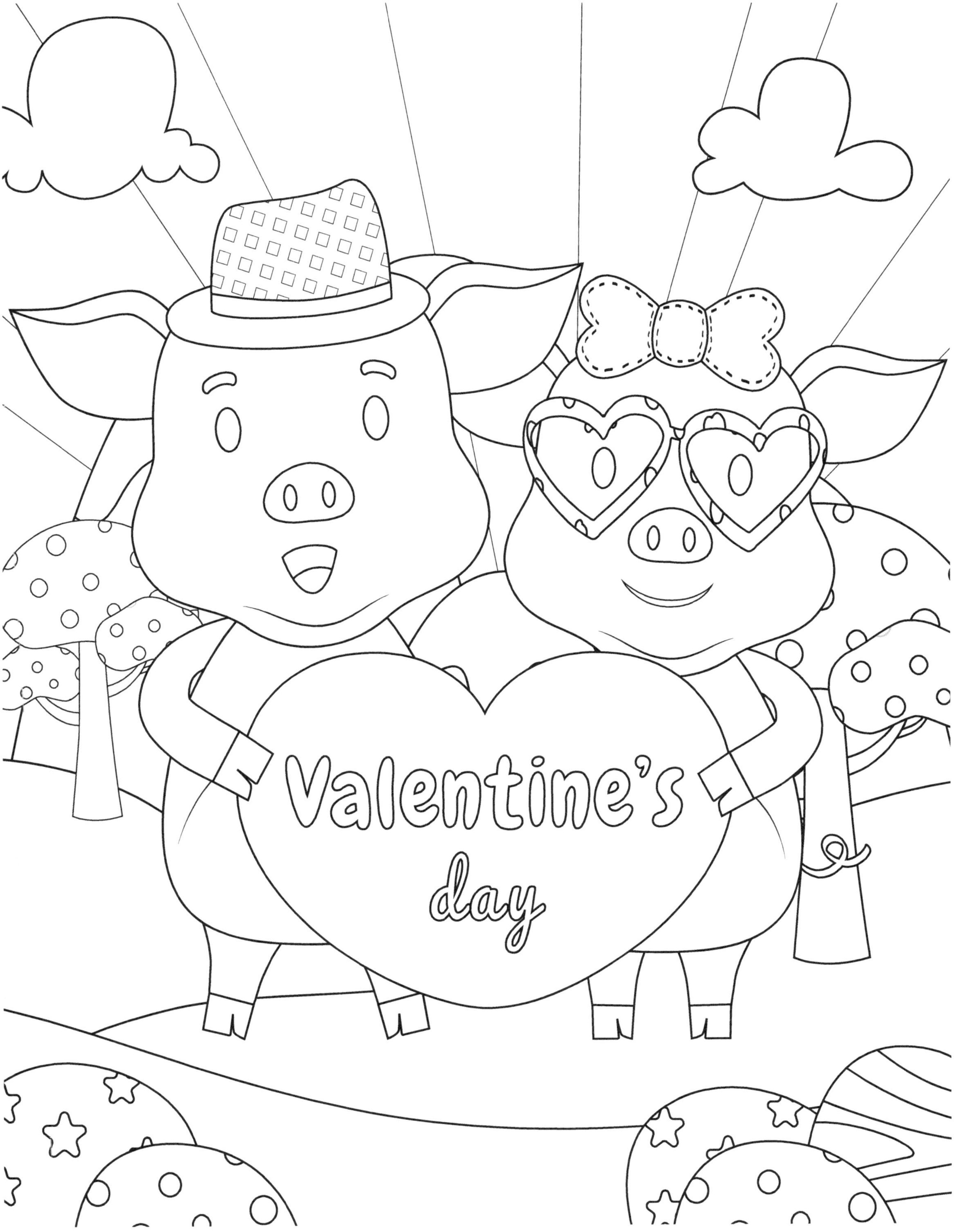
Valentine's
day

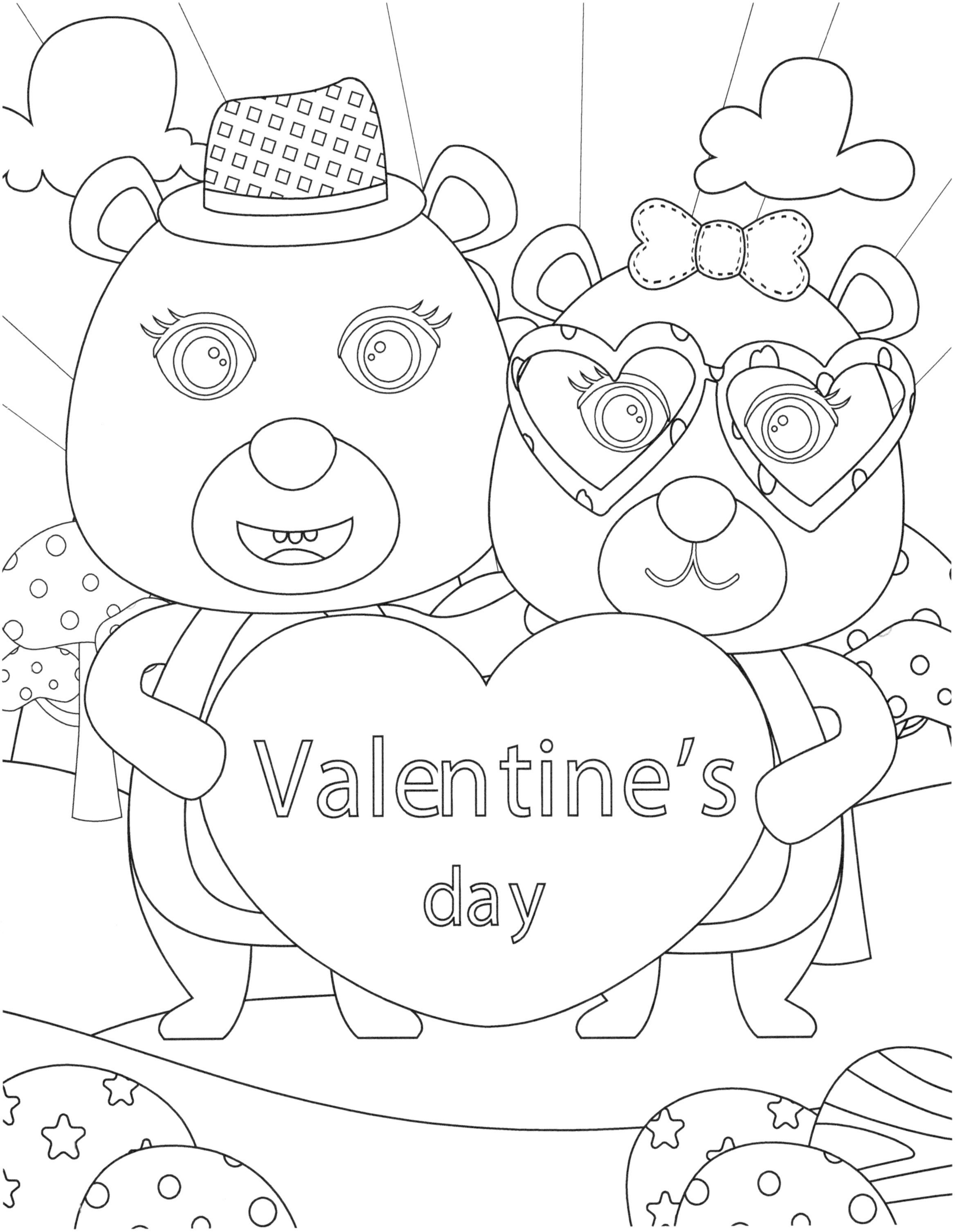
Valentine's
day

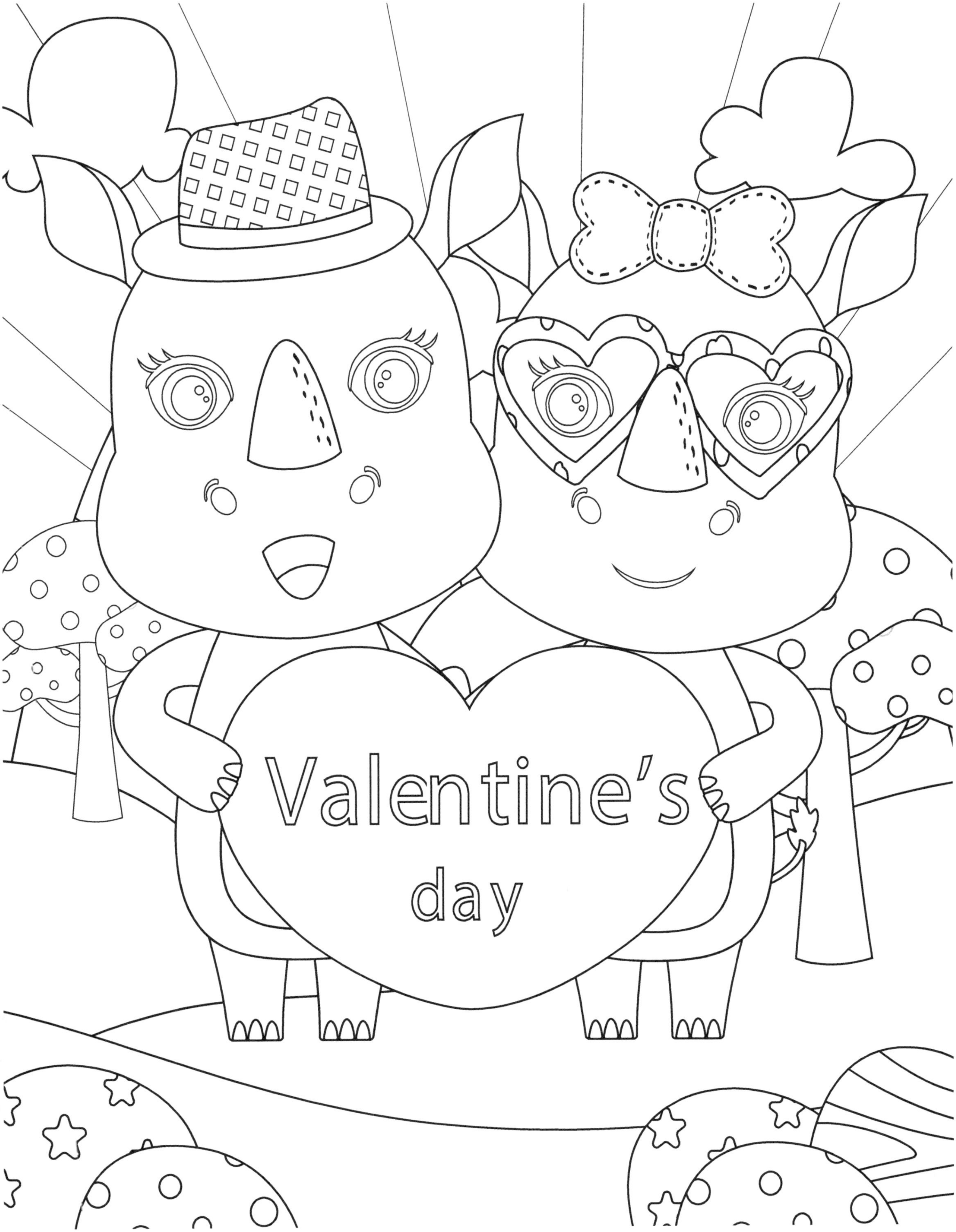
Valentine's
day

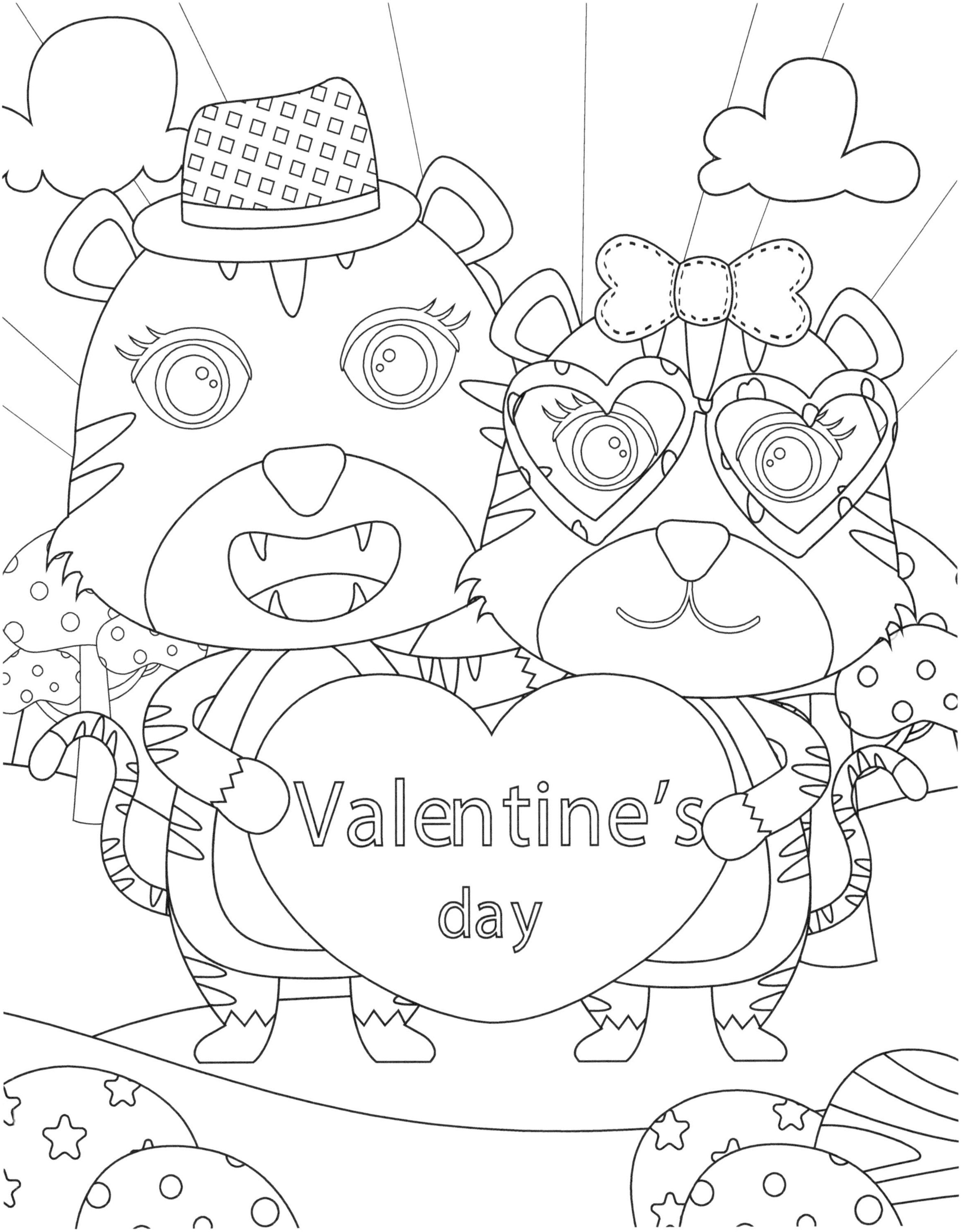
Valentine's
day

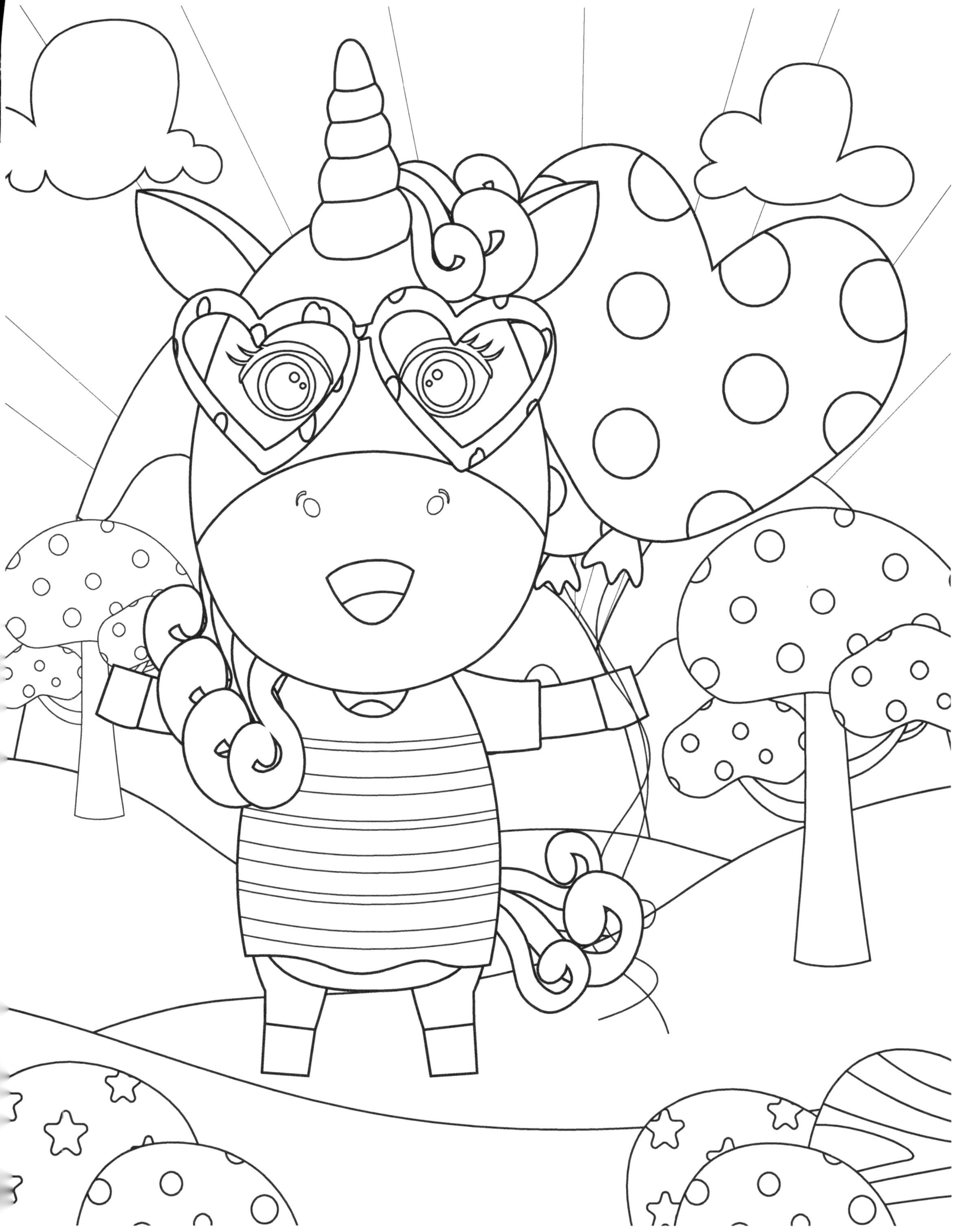

www.ingramcontent.com/pod-product-compliance
Lightning Source LLC
Chambersburg PA
CBHW081520220526
45467CB00010B/2986
9798707062414